The School Governors' Hand

Third edition

The pace of change in education has continued to accelerate since the 1988 Education Act. As governors rarely receive any specific training, even experienced school governors are often bewildered about their duties and responsibilities, as well as what is actually happening in primary and secondary classrooms. What do school governors do? How can they manage their role most effectively?

The School Governors' Handbook has been the most definitive and widely read book on the subject since it was first published in 1980. Written by Ted Wragg and John Partington, two of the most respected experts in the field, one of its great strengths has always been its mixture of up-to-date, authoritative information and humour. Now in its third edition, all sections of the book have been substantially revised and rewritten to take account of the many changes in governors' duties that have been brought about by recent legislation.

Sections cover:
- recent legislative changes in funding and school management;
- opting out;
- governors' responsibilities, including budgets, staffing and drawing up; whole school policies;
- how to run an effective governors' meeting;
- curriculum, assessment and what happens in the classroom;
- school inspections;
- how to manage difficult situations and issues, including child protection, discipline, equal opportunities and pupil exclusions.

Ted Wragg will be familiar to readers from his widespread writing, including his regular column in *The Times Educational Supplement*, and many books. He is also Professor of Education at the University of Exeter. **John Partington** was formerly Vice-Dean of the Faculty of Education at the University of Nottingham, and has also published widely. He is currently a governor of three schools.

The School Governors' Handbook

Third edition

E. C. Wragg and J. A. Partington

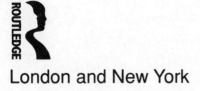

London and New York

First published 1980 by Methuen & Co Ltd
Second edition by Routledge 1989
11 New Fetter Lane, London EC4P 4EE

Reprinted 1990

Third edition published 1995 by Routledge

Simultaneously published in the USA and Canada
by Routledge
29 West 35th Street, New York, NY 10001

Typeset in Garamond by
Ponting–Green Publishing Services, Chesham, Bucks

Printed and bound in Great Britain by
TJ Press (Padstow) Ltd, Padstow, Cornwall

British Library Cataloguing in Publication Data
A catalogue record for this book is available from the
British Library.

Library of Congress Cataloguing in Publication Data
A catalogue record for this book has been requested.

ISBN 0–415–12707–6

Contents

Figures

Acknowledgements

Acknowledgement is gratefully expressed for material from the following publications:

Figure 1   Butler, P., Carrington, D. and Ellis, G. (1986) *Science Watch*, Cambridge: Cambridge University Press.

Figure 2   Ted Wragg (1994) *Flying Boot*, London: Thomas Nelson.

Figure 3   Roy Holland (1992) *Ginn Mathematics 6+*, Ginn and Company Ltd.

Figure 4   John Holman (1994) *Science World: Teacher's Resource Book 2*, London: Thomas Nelson. Series visualised and illustrated by Val Biro.

Figure 5   Sylvia Honnor, Ron Holt and Heather Mascie-Taylor (1980) *Tricolore*, Stage One, Pupils' Book, E.J. Arnold.

Figure 6   Maura Healy (1981) *Your Language Two*, London and Basingstoke: Macmillan.

Figure 7   Ted Wragg (1994) *Flying Boot*, London: Thomas Nelson.

Figure 8   John Blackie (1974) *Changing the Primary School*, London: Macmillan.

Cartoons   by Jon Hall.

Introduction

You can recognise school governors quite easily nowadays. They are the ones hurrying along clutching a large wad of papers, wearing the slightly hunted look of a fugitive master spy. A few years ago their counterparts would have been anonymous, relaxed people who only turned up at their school once in a while for a cup of tea and a biscuit, followed by a short session largely devoted to deciding the date and time of the next meeting. Since the 1980s school governors have held one of the most important voluntary jobs in our society.

Whereas in former times governors had few powers, successive Acts of Parliament have given them more and more say in what happens in schools. By the end of the 1980s they had effectively become the employers of teaching and non-teaching staff, with a budget that could exceed a million pounds. Their responsibilities had become significant. In the case of the curriculum alone, they found themselves trying to understand what goes on in ten or more different subjects. This was especially difficult at a time of massive changes in the education of primary and secondary school children.

We have written this book for ordinary people, many of whom may become a school governor for the first time. Most governors are volunteers of one kind or another, though this will raise a hollow laugh from those who were coerced, cajoled, co-opted or even conned into becoming a governor. ('It's an important job. There shouldn't be too many meetings . . .' Ha ha. Pull the other one.) This is now the third edition, and we have tried to revise everything completely to make sure that the contents are as informative, authoritative and up to date as possible.

We have been involved in the training of governors for over twenty years, and we have found that, despite the many changes in the education system, governors' needs are fairly consistent. Amongst the questions most commonly asked are:

- How can I help the school?
- Where can I find out more about what happens in schools?
- What is expected of me when I am appointed?

- I am a parent (or teacher). How can I best serve the people who elected me?
- How does a committee work?
- What are governors supposed to do if a really tricky situation arises?
- Where can we turn for help if we don't understand a particular matter?
- Can governors actually get something done?

These questions have guided us in our choice of topics for the chapters in this book.

We recognise that some governors may already be very knowledgeable about the education system. Teacher governors actually work in classrooms, so they have valuable first-hand information and experience of many of the matters that come up in meetings. People who have served on other committees in their jobs, in voluntary organisations, in the county or town hall, will often know a great deal about the procedures and conventions of committee meetings. Some people's experience of bringing up their own children and of family needs and aspirations, of working in different jobs, or experience with young people of varying social backgrounds, also represents useful expertise. Putting your knowledge, experience and good sense at the disposal of your fellow governors, rather than blinding them with science, is one of the most important contributions anyone can make on a governing body.

The two most important features of successful school governors are:

1 a concern for the well-being of the children, teachers and others in the school community
2 commonsense

Given these two attributes in sufficient quantity amongst membership of the governing body, many problems can eventually be solved.

IS BEING A GOVERNOR A WASTE OF TIME?

Sadly some governors' meetings appear so tedious and pointless they make Samuel Beckett's pause-laden play *Waiting for Godot* look like the chariot race in *Ben Hur*. At the end members, their brains corroded beyond redemption, decide to go home and do something really interesting, like counting the pages in the telephone directory. But being a governor should not be a waste of time, even if some meetings are a bit boring. If meetings become frustrating it is up to the members, especially the person chairing them, to try to work out why this is happening. Is nobody interested in what goes on in the school? Is the agenda too full of trivial routine matters with no opportunity to discuss important issues? If so then appropriate steps can and should be taken.

To some extent the title 'Governor' may be unhelpful. It suggests the holder goes around giving orders to people, an image which may sometimes cause antagonism, especially with teachers. In real life governors actually give very few orders as such. Their function is not to run the school on a day-to-day basis, but rather to keep an eye on it, help sort out problems, influence the general direction of policy and practice, and get the best possible deal from outside agencies. In our view the best partnerships between professionals and lay people are based on mutual respect. The lay people respect the professional judgement of the head and teachers, and the professionals respect the views and concerns of lay people like parents and members of the community. We have come across a few examples of this partnership working badly, but an overwhelming number of instances of it working well.

There could be plenty of scope for aggravation. After all, education has become a high profile activity, often discussed in the press and on radio and television, with some accusations that certain children are being short-changed and receiving a poor standard of education. There is a strong sense of accountability in our society, and schools, like any other institutions receiving public money, must be open to scrutiny by representatives of the wider community. Sensible governors fulfil this role by taking the trouble to find out what is actually happening in their own school, rather than merely believing what they read in the papers, which may or may not be a true account of what is taking place on their own patch. They then use their imagination, knowledge and energy to see what they can do to support effective teaching and learning in their school.

THE PURPOSE OF THIS BOOK

Nobody reading a single book can become an expert overnight in a field as complex as education. Even those who work professionally as teachers, heads, inspectors, support staff, or advisers and administrators, find that they can learn new things about education throughout their professional lives. No one has it sewn up. So we hope that those who take the trouble to read this book will be in a better position to play a full part in governors' meetings, because they will understand more fully what is going on in the school.

We begin, therefore, in Chapters 1 and 2, by concentrating on how governors fit into the educational system, what the job entails, what they are expected and empowered to do. In Chapter 3 we look in more detail at individual governors, be they parents, teachers, nominations from the local authority, or co-opted members, showing how each can make a significant contribution. How a committee actually works is another matter of universal importance to governors, and Chapter 4 covers committee workings, group dynamics, and the use of dirty tricks, which is a topic rarely covered in books like this.

Many governors want to know more about life in the classroom and how a school works from the inside. In Chapters 5 and 6 we discuss life in school and some of the central issues in education. We can only prick the surface of this complex and intricate world, but we try to whet governors' appetite for discovering more about the challenges and problems of teaching and learning in schools today. Often it is the problems which perplex a governing body, so finally, in Chapter 7, we take a look at thorny issues which have taxed governors, like pupil suspensions (now called 'exclusions'), accidents and vandalism.

AN OPTIMISTIC/REALISTIC VIEW

We take as our starting point the optimistic belief that most governors are trying to be helpful. It is, of course, true that some are not, that certain governors may even be arch-villains, enemies of humanity. A senior police-man once said that master criminals were so well disguised in our society, they had taken on respectable roles and that some were even school governors. There is no section in this book on safe-cracking or running a protection racket to increase school funds, however, as we are writing for Mr and Mrs Little, not Mr Big.

It is also our firm belief that most teachers and heads are committed to the well-being of the children and parents in their school. We have worked in and visited hundreds of schools, and though we come across a few in-competent teachers who are a menace and should be got rid of, the vast majority are doing their best, often in difficult circumstances. We concentrate on trying to establish a *positive relationship* between governors and teachers, in the belief that this is best for all concerned.

We hope that readers of this book will find education as interesting as we do ourselves. We have both attended conferences where ashen-faced edu-cators proclaim gloom and doom, and have read our fill of jargon-laden papers in which lessons have become 'sequences of learning experiences' and simple toys are transformed into 'learning stimulus materials'. We have kept the professional jargon to a minimum, as we assume that most readers want to enjoy being a governor, not train as barristers. If some of our descriptions are occasionally written in a lighthearted vein, then this is because human behaviour in general, and events in school in particular, can often be funny, pretentiousness and pomposity being especially hilarious.

There are four final points we wish to make in this introductory section. The first is that no book can be completely up to date. A change of government, new Acts of Parliament or fresh policies can soon reverse a situation that has operated for years. We describe the state of play at the time of writing. We have included in this third edition information about the major Acts of Parliament and changes in the National Curriculum as they are in the mid-1990s.

Our second point is that we have concentrated on primary and secondary schools in the state system, which are attended by over 90 per cent of children.

Much of what we describe is relevant to governors of colleges of further education, even though these are now independent of local authorities, and to governors of special, denominational, or independent schools. In Chapter 1 we refer specifically to being a governor in some of these different schools.

Our third point is that we usually write in the plural about governors, teacher, parents or pupils, but when we write in the singular we sometimes use 'she' and other times 'he', to avoid giving the impression that all key positions or events involve men and boys. Fourthly, governors of schools in Scotland and Northern Ireland will sometimes find variations in practice from what we describe, which is the current situation in England and Wales. These differences are usually, however, only slight.

Chapter 1

How governors fit into the education system

When governors are appointed, they usually want to know the answers to questions such as: How do schools work? What power do I have? What can I do? What can I *not* do? We attempt to answer some of these questions here.

WHO'S IN CHARGE?

The short answer of course is that Parliament is supreme and can do whatever it wants to do in education whenever it sees fit – and it must be said that since 1980 it has been very busy indeed, as most readers will be aware from the press. There have been several major Acts of Parliament and a vast number of detailed regulations based on them. The Secretary of State for Education is a member of the Cabinet. He or she heads the relevant government department in London. The department used to be called the 'Department of Education and Science', but was then renamed the 'Department for Education' (DFE), on the grounds perhaps that it was better to be *for* education than *against* it.

The Secretary of State is required by law to 'promote the education of the people of England and Wales', and has power to 'direct' any local education authority or school governing body to act 'reasonably' if it is feared that they are going off the rails. This does not mean, however, that Secretaries of State can play the dictator and stop developments simply because they disagree with them. They should only act over something which 'the man on the Clapham omnibus' would think *unreasonable*, to quote Lord Denning in the High Court. It should also be said that Secretaries of State only rarely make use of this legal sledgehammer, preferring instead to persuade and cajole.

When the earlier editions of this book were written in the 1980s, we could still talk about some sort of equal partnership in education between the Department for Education, school governing bodies and local education authorities. Since the early 1990s this is much less the case. There has been a considerable shift of power away from local education authorities towards school governing bodies and towards the Department for Education, so much so that there is real concern about the future of local education authorities.

Some people fear that the public accountability of schools will be lost if local education authorities disappear, others argue that nothing could exemplify local government *better* than locally elected and appointed school governing bodies consisting of parents, teachers and others with a real interest in their own school. It was, sadly, the case at one time that local education authority representatives on governing bodies were caricatured popularly as sleeping through most governors' meetings, stirring only to raise their voting hand in favour (sometimes both hands) when the chair (usually of the same political party) gave them some pre-arranged cue.

These changes have come about through legislation which requires local education authorities to delegate budgets to schools and give governors responsibility for spending the money. Since the 1988 Education Act parents can even vote for their school to sever almost all links within their local education authorities, a process known as 'opting out'. If they do, their school becomes a 'grant maintained' school and receives its funding directly from the Department for Education. We return to these themes later.

School governors nowadays carry a lot of new responsibilities and work very hard. There is talk of governor stress and drop-out. Jokes about schools providing folding beds for exhausted governors after weekly meetings are only a bit far-fetched. That said, very many enjoy the new challenges and it is clear that a new breed of governor is emerging, particularly governors with business interests (very useful for matters to do with budgeting), catering interests (the school meals budget can sometimes make or break a school), governors with a strong interest in ensuring that schools relate well to their local communities. There are also governors with professional knowledge about schools and education, who can make a real contribution alongside the head teacher and teaching staff, without feeling squeezed out by 'local education authority policy'.

These changes hit governing bodies very suddenly and quickly in the late 1980s and governors were by and large caught unawares. The demand for governor training grew, and local education authorities were put into the unenviable position of having to provide training which would have the effect of doing themselves out of much of their work.

These changes have also brought problems. Despite enjoying their new status in the education system, governors have become aware that without specialist local education authority staff, such as school inspectors, subject teaching advisers, administrators, accountants and legal experts, many of whose jobs at County Hall have disappeared, they can have difficulty getting day-to-day advice when they need it. This is why governors who have relevant expertise are much sought after. Employment law, for example, is a tricky area, and governors are nowadays responsible for hiring, firing and paying staff.

An issue which one suspects that the government did not foresee was that, however keen governors are, *someone* has to 'police' the system as local education authorities used to do. This is in no way to suggest that governors are criminals, but rather that innocence and ignorance combined can entrap even the most sincere and devoted. People who feel angry, cheated or defrauded by what school governors do on occasion can take legal action like any citizen. But this is time-consuming and expensive and cannot compare with a phone call or visit to the local education authority or a local councillor, who, as often as not, could put right small things at least, quickly and with a minimum of fuss.

As this situation has emerged, so the Department for Education itself has had to take on more and more and more of this work. It has abolished for the most part Her Majesty's Inspectors of Schools (usually known as HMI) who used to be the eyes, ears and trouble-shooters of the Department for Education. The mainstream staff of the Department for Education have little first-hand experience of schools and do not pay regular visits as HMI widely used to do. They can operate only through a stream of regulations called Statutory Instruments, which actually form part of the law of the land. It is doubtful whether the Department for Education is nowadays as well informed about what is going on in the nation's schools as it used to be. Some of the bureaucracy and accompanying regulations appearing would be hilarious if they were not so serious.

Keeping up with all these is a time-consuming part of a governor's work, although by using a system of governors' sub-committees each with its own specialist area the burden can be shared. Governors then need to know only those regulations which affect their immediate work. All governors should ensure that they have access to copies of these regulations: a good idea is to get the governing body to invest in a volume containing all the regulations – and preferably a loose-leaf volume which can be up-dated quickly. There should be one available at every meeting.

To give an idea of the areas covered by regulations, here are a few gripping titles:

Education (Special Educational Needs) Regulations 1983
Education (School Records) Regulations 1989
Education (School Government) Regulations 1989
Education (Areas to which Pupils and Students Belong) Regulations 1989
Education (School Teacher Appraisal) Regulations 1991
Education (School Inspection) Regulations 1993

There are also literally *dozens* of sets of regulations about the National Curriculum and various subjects within it, which maintained ('state') schools have been obliged to follow since the Education Act of 1988. Governors can safely leave most of these to head teachers and teaching staff, although any governor with a particular interest is very welcome to indulge in a bit of bedtime reading. They are just as effective as sleeping pills and less harmful: some teachers even find them a good laugh. There is a lot of truth in the old saying that a group of experts together can be as dotty as anyone else. In 1994 the National Curriculum was made simpler, and we deal with that matter in Chapter 5.

WHAT DO LOCAL EDUCATION AUTHORITIES DO?

Although their powers have been reduced, local education authorities still do have responsibilities. Some of the duties which they used to carry out have been transferred from them to the Funding Agency for Schools (FAS) which came into being in April 1994. This body was set up to administer the funding for the grant maintained schools. However it is obvious that in any area where there are large numbers of grant maintained schools, there is a danger that local education authorities and the Funding Agency would start to fall over each other, hence the need for the Secretary of State to decide who does what. Very briefly then, the traditional duties of local education authorities are to:

- *Ensure that there are enough school places available for their area.* They do not have to make all the places available in their own schools. They can make arrangements with independent schools in their area, but must pay the fees if they do. It is only the *total number* of places which is important. Parents cannot insist on a school place in a particular part of town or in, say, a denominational school.
- *Finance their schools.* The Education Acts never say anything directly about how well local education authorities must finance their schools, however. That is left to local and national politics, although some expenditure – teachers' salaries, for example – is laid down nationally by law, and local education authorities and governors would get into trouble by failing to spend accordingly.
- *Under certain circumstances provide pupils with free transport to school.*
- *Ensure that all children in their area are educated.* Notice that the law does not require children *to go to school:* parents can make any arrangements they like to educate their children, but they must satisfy the local education authority that their children are being properly educated.
- *Make sure that schools receive their delegated budget funds.*
- *Make sure that the National Curriculum is fully taught.* Incidentally, pupils do not have a *right* to be taught according to the National Curriculum: local education authorities have a *duty* to provide it. If a local education authority could satisfy the Secretary of State that it cannot provide all or part of the National Curriculum, then the disappointed pupils would be helpless.
- *Ensure that religious education takes place and that pupils attend.*
- *Ensure that pupils with special educational needs are suitably cared for.*
- *Ensure that there are facilities for pupils to eat meals and other refreshments.*

Local education authorities since 1980 do not have to provide the meals or refreshment if they do not wish.

- *Make arrangements for medical and dental checks.*
- *Arrange for parents to express preferences about which school they would like their child to attend.* Parental choice of school has turned out to be a tricky area since it was formally introduced in 1980. It is certainly a good thing that local education authorities must ask all parents what they would like. There can be no guarantee, however, that parents will be granted their choice. Governors of popular and over-subscribed schools are frequently involved in explaining how they choose children from all those who apply (schools must have so-called 'admissions criteria'). Disappointed parents can also appeal and governors can be involved as members of Appeals Panels which local education authorities must set up as and when needed.

  Incidentally, lawyers are increasingly concerned that the right to choose a curriculum and to appeal over exclusion are given to parents, but not to pupils themselves. One wonders how many pupils are put at a disadvantage by what their parents do in these respects. An intelligent young teenager could be forced into an unsuitable education by intransigent parents *without even the right to be consulted.* Readers of biographies will be aware of how many well-known figures had this experience.
- *Provide a careers service.* Advice on careers is usually available within each school, but the local education authority can provide careers advice to all.

DIFFERENT TYPES OF SCHOOL

Over 90 per cent of children go to local primary and secondary schools which are funded out of public money. Yet all schools are not the same. Decisions about the form which schooling should take have often been made at local level. That is why there is such a variety of schools in the United Kingdom, compared with many other countries which have a uniform type of provision. The origins of certain kinds of school lie deep in the past. Other schools are of more recent vintage. Most of this book is aimed at governors in local authority maintained primary and secondary schools. However, there are thousands of governors of independent and other types of school which are outside the control of the local authorities, so we go into a little more detail below about being a governor of such other schools.

Voluntary schools

Voluntary schools are the direct descendants of schools which were going concerns before Parliament began to take an interest in education during the nineteenth century. Originally these schools were self-supporting and re-ceived their funds from fees, bequests, endowments and any other available sources. As the state system of schools expanded it became clear that the places in those schools were vitally necessary to ensure education for all. At the same time the value of the schools' assets was dwindling (often they had old, out-moded buildings) and their original endowments were being eaten away by inflation, so that some form of government subsidy became both desirable and necessary. Since 1902 the financial responsibility for these schools has rested with local education authorities and they are included in the school places which local education authorities must make available for their area.

As a governor of a voluntary school you will find then that your school is owned not by the local education authority but by a trust or charity representing the original owners, going back perhaps hundreds of years. Years ago the churches and monarchs often founded schools (Henry the Eighth founded Eton College), as did craft guilds (Coopers, Tanners, Haberdashers and Merchant Taylors, for example) and many wealthy individuals. Somewhere in the office of the clerk to the governors there will be an old trust deed explaining your founder's intentions for the school.

Some members of your governing body will be called 'foundation governors'. On top of all their other obligations as governors they are there to ensure that as many of the founder's intentions as are still possible shall continue, regardless of how long ago they were created. It is not possible here to list all the things you might find: most commonly there may be a requirement that the school should teach the Jewish, Anglican or Roman Catholic faith or that your pupils should come from a particular area. As well as attending all routine governors' meetings, foundation governors often have separate meetings of their own. They must make sure that 'the character of the school as a voluntary school is preserved and developed and, in particular, that the school is conducted in accordance with the provisions of any trust deed relating thereto'.

There are three types of voluntary school. If you are a governor of a *voluntary aided* school, you and your colleagues are responsible for finding the money to keep the buildings of your school well maintained, decorated and repaired – although the Department for Education in Whitehall will at present refund 85 per cent of the costs to you. In the same way, if you make the decision to enlarge your buildings, or perhaps move to a better site (voluntary schools sometimes find nowadays that there are insufficient pupils close by because they are in inner-city areas), 85 per cent of the costs can be reclaimed if the Department for Education believes that what you are doing is justified.

A *voluntary controlled* school may well have started its life very much in the same way as a voluntary aided school, but found with the passage of time that it could not manage the financial commitments of an aided school. The local education authority will therefore have agreed to take over all the expenses of the school. There will still be foundation governors as in aided schools.

Special agreement schools were established as a 'one-off job' in the later 1930s, and local authorities paid between 50 per cent and 75 per cent of the cost of establishing them. None has been set up since and no more are likely to be. Being a governor of one of these schools is to all intents and purposes like being the governor of an aided school.

There is often controversy over whether other religious schools, like Muslim schools, should be admitted to the education system as voluntary schools. It is hard to see why other faiths should be admitted and the Muslim community be denied. In any case, following its election in 1992, the Conservative government tried to make it easier for interest groups to be able to set up their own schools. Apart from differences of local detail, the obligations of local education authorities towards aided schools are as listed above, and governors must co-operate with them.

Grant maintained schools

This type of school, sometimes called an 'opted out school', came into being for the first time in the Education Reform Act of 1988. They have been and are still controversial. Briefly, if a school wishes to leave the control of its local authority, then a ballot must be held amongst parents of the school. If over 50 per cent of them vote and there is a majority in favour of 'opting out', as it is popularly known, then a school can sever most of its links with its local education authority and be funded directly, since April 1994, by the Funding Agency for Schools. In that case the governors take over full responsibility for the running of the school.

Some believe that the principle of 'opting out' is fundamentally mis-conceived. They argue that if the idea really catches on then an impossible situation will arise. Local education authorities will go into even more rapid decline. The Funding Agency and the Department for Education will be left with the overall supervision of 20,000+ individual schools, which will rapidly lead to chaos without a dramatic expansion of central bureaucracy. The Funding Agency for Schools, set up in 1994, is an example. Moreover schools will be encouraged to compete with each other for pupils and resources. Some are very unhappy to see consumerism applied to schools as it is applied to shops.

Opponents further argue that local authorities are also responsible for helping their employees to improve by providing training courses and advisory services which inject new ideas into schools. It is hard to see where such initiatives can come from if local authorities are gradually run down. Furthermore, since schools *do not start equal* in their premises, traditions, funding and general attractiveness, those that are already strong will become even stronger, and the weaker become even weaker, a situation which local education authorities, not always successfully, it must be said, have existed to prevent.

Supporters say that some schools have got on badly with their local education authorities, and governors have been dispirited by policies, attitudes and efficiency at some county and town halls. At times quite bitter party political issues have been fought on school governing bodies, and non-political governors have had to look on bemused, or find themselves inevitably out-voted on these time-consuming issues. Sometimes, too, well-intentioned local education authority policies have seemed irrelevant and costly to governors trying to run their school in the best way on less than adequate funds. 'Opting out' has been welcomed by such governing bodies and their parents, and many, though not all, of the first grant maintained schools have been popular and successful. Few, it is said, wish to return to their local education authority – assuming, that is, that the authority would welcome them, since relationships after 'opting out' have sometimes not been easy.

If a ballot shows that parents would like the school to be grant maintained, a formal application must be made to the Secretary of State. Acceptance is not automatic, though so far most bids have been successful. As far as parents' rights are concerned grant maintained schools are like local education authority schools. There are no fees and they do not generally change from being comprehensive or grammar schools because they have left the local education authority. Fears that many comprehensives would immediately wish to become selective schools were in general misplaced, though a few have changed their entrance policies and decided to take more able children.

There is a widely held belief that some grant maintained schools have shed their most disruptive pupils in order to smarten up their image. But some local education authority schools, after the introduction of local management for schools, have done the same thing and the government legislated in 1993 to give authorities power to make governors admit pupils who might otherwise be left to roam the streets.

Whether a school decides to opt out depends on a whole host of local circumstances. Some were moved by the belief that more generous funding was available at the time they applied. The Department for Education response was that grant maintained schools may have to 'buy in' services provided free by local authorities and therefore needed more cash. Some schools, facing closure because of falling pupil numbers or local education authority financial cuts, became grant maintained, but others, especially small schools, despite a positive result in the ballot, were turned down by the Department for Education because of a potential waste of resources. A few schools without sixth forms opted out in order to establish one. Some schools sought generous technology grants which at first were only made available by the Conservative government to those that had opted out.

Governors must by law once a year consider whether they wish to opt out. Since 1993 they are permitted to promote the idea of grant maintained status. In their annual report to parents they must confirm that they have considered holding a ballot of parents and give reasons for their decision. If they have not discussed the matter, this too must be explained. Normally governors decide on their own agenda but this item is compulsory. It must be discussed by a full and quorate governors' meeting. It cannot be referred to a sub-committee or left to chair's action.

In making their decision about grant maintained status governors need to be aware of the changes to their work which it would bring. Here are some of the things which grant maintained schools have to set up for themselves or pay others to do for them:

- cleaning services
- catering services
- employment contracts for all types of staff
- instrumental music tuition
- library services
- caretaking and maintenance provision
- commissioning building plans and surveying
- wages and salaries to all staff
- school inspections
- regular appraisal of all staff
- backup on legal matters
- accounting and auditing

The list looks formidable, but many governing bodies of grant maintained schools have coped with the extra responsibility. Your decision may also be influenced by factors like:

- the expertise (present and future) available amongst the governors
- the changes or developments you seek for your school
- how unanimous the governing body is about the proposed changes
- how far the governing body is willing to undertake the extra time commitment it would bring
- the attitude of the head and staff. While there is no legal obligation to *consult* staff, apart from talking to your head teacher and teacher governors at meetings, there is much to be said for getting their enthusiastic co-operation

City technology colleges

In pursuing its policy of offering parents a wider range of schools, the government, through the 1988 Education Act, also introduced city technology colleges. Like grant maintained schools these have been controversial. The thinking behind CTCs as they are popularly known is that government and industry should work together to introduce a much more substantial element of technology into the school curriculum, and to make schools more responsive to the country's economic needs. This is another attempt to get to grips with a very long-standing issue in UK education: other governments have tackled it in different ways, with only moderate success.

The government in 1988 resurrected an old UK tradition by which individuals or firms put up money for schools. Many readers, particularly in the North of England, will recognise that the schools they attended years ago often bore the name of some benefactor and founders, probably from the nineteenth century. In the case of CTCs it was agreed that any additional funding needed would be provided by the government. Critics of the CTCs were quick to point out that private investment was not as much as had been hoped and that the government and the taxpayer had been obliged to come up with more. The sponsors have been individuals, charitable foundations, large firms and high street stores. A change of policy was introduced in 1994: local authorities could, if they wished, convert an existing school into a CTC – it then became a voluntary aided CTC as described above.

One advantage enjoyed by CTCs, particularly those built or staffed from new, is that they are much more open to breaking tradition and can more easily experiment. 'Breaking the mould' is an expression frequently heard about CTCs. They can have new styles of management, and can try new curriculum ideas, although they are obliged to teach the National Curriculum for the first three years. They can employ staff on such terms and conditions of service as may be agreed, and are not necessarily bound by national agreements. Some have moved to a four-term year, some work a longer school day, some encourage pupils into business experience at an early age by selling goods produced at the college such as pottery. Throughout the curriculum runs the theme of technology: computer-based learning is very prominent.

Critics point to the relatively lavish funding for CTCs and the relatively poor reports from early inspections about the teaching of science and technology in some of the CTCs. Local authorities argue that *they* should have been given the funding for technological education. They also point to the amount of money – much less – which they have to spend on local authority schools. The government view, however, is that it has no power to *direct* how local authorities spend their money (the sense of independence of local government is strong) and that previous attempts to encourage local authorities to spend on new types of school curriculum have not been overwhelmingly successful. The government also has a strong card to play, in that CTCs are meant to serve inner-city areas and are part of inner-city regeneration policies, of which of course most undoubtedly approve. CTCs are also intended to enhance technological education for *average* pupils, leaving other types of school to look after the high-flyers.

The first CTCs were 11–18 comprehensive schools taking their pupils from the immediate area of the college. The newer ones, however, are free to recruit from wherever they like. Like grant maintained schools they are funded directly from the Department for Education and their day-to-day funding is related to the amount the local authority for their area chooses to spend on its own schools, thus removing a potential point of friction.

The nature of CTCs suggests that their governors should come from industry, commerce and the professions. Parents are also consulted. The 1988 Act does not specify exactly who should form part of the governing body. Usually, as in voluntary schools, there are foundation governors, more often called trustees. There are some disagreements between the major political parties about the nature and continued existence of both grant maintained schools and CTCs, and these may well affect their development. There was such rapid change in education in the 1980s and 1990s, affecting all types of school, not just the mainstream local authority schools, that governors of schools outside the local authority network need to be particularly vigilant about what is happening.

Independent schools

Independent schools are very much like businesses, selling education through fees paid by parents at a price the market will stand. One of the underlying trends in all types of school over the last few years has been to make their management more like that of independent schools, with the important difference, of course, that only independent schools may by law charge fees. A high proportion of independent schools are boarding schools or have a small boarding house if most of their pupils are day pupils. Many cities have large independent day schools, usually single-sex, usually selective in some way and usually geared primarily to academic success.

Whereas other schools of all types are regulated to a greater or lesser degree by the Department for Education or the Funding Agency for Schools, independent schools are largely free to develop their own policy and practice alongside other schools. Governors of independent schools tend to restrict their activity to the economic affairs of the school, leaving much more to the unfettered judgement of their head teacher, whereas in other schools the law involves governors formally in major areas of school policy. In boarding schools it is difficult for governors to have meaningful contacts with parents who live a very long way away. Nevertheless governors of independent schools are, in law, responsible for *everything* which happens at the school – including the misdemeanours of their head teacher if they occur.

Independent schools, apart from those which are privately owned, are registered charities and as such are responsible to the Charities Commission for the proper conduct of their affairs. Accounts, for example, have to be submitted. They must also be registered with the Department for Education, and there is a Registrar of Independent Schools. They are open to inspection by the Office for Standards in Education (OFSTED), like other schools. Should it become necessary, the Independent Schools Tribunal is empowered to put a school out of business: the owner of a private school can be declared an unfit person to run a school and banned. A teacher can be declared unfit to teach in any school.

Increasingly the law is taking a hand in the affairs of independent schools in a number of ways. The Charities Acts of 1992 and 1993 have greatly strengthened the powers of the Charity Commissioners to require accounts to be presented in certain ways, and more closely to control the purchase and selling of assets. If the school closes there is the possibility that governors individually *may* be liable for outstanding debts – something against which sensible independent school governors insure themselves.

Corporal punishment was banned in all schools except independent schools in 1986. Cynics commented that if parents wanted their child beaten in school, they would now have to pay for it. However the legal ban on corporal punishment extends to pupils in independent schools whose fees are subsidised by the Assisted Places scheme. This fact alone has served to eliminate more vestiges of corporal punishment in independent schools, since no school can live comfortably with two distinct classes of pupil – those who may receive corporal punishment and those who may not. Moreover the Education Act of 1993 has gone further and ruled illegal any punishment in independent schools which is 'inhuman or degrading', quoting the European Convention on Human Rights.

Horror stories of child abuse nationally have also had their effect. The 1989 Children Act sought to protect children in children's homes, thus raising the issue of whether a boarding school is a children's home. If a boarding school is classified as a children's home, it – and the pupils in it – must be extensively visited and supervised by the social services department of the local authority. To avoid this, a boarding school, under the Education Act of 1993, must try to ensure that it allows no more than three pupils to remain in the school for more than 295 days in any two consecutive years. This can create difficulties for boarding schools which have numbers of pupils whose parents live abroad or are constantly on the move. Such parents frequently seek to have their children remain in school at least partly during the vacations. Schools or pupils' parents now have to find guardians to be responsible for pupils' welfare during vacations.

WHO CAN BE A GOVERNOR?

All sorts of people may become governors. If you are reasonably sane, solvent, and not in jail, you are probably eligible. Independent schools and city technology colleges can choose whomsoever they want. For all other schools the guidelines are:

- *Parents of children at the school.* They must be elected by a properly organised secret postal ballot.
- *Representatives of the local education authority.* These are usually elected councillors, but the law does not say that they must be. Some authorities appoint representatives who have no political affiliations, others insist on,

or much prefer, people who belong to the same political party as is in control at city or county hall.

- *The head teacher* can choose whether or not to be a governor. Most become a full governor, though some prefer to see themselves as the governors' chief executive. Governor or not, the head teacher is always entitled to attend all governors' meetings. Most heads prefer to be governors, so that they can, for example, have a vote in the appointment of staff.
- *Teacher governors* are elected by their colleagues.
- *Foundation governors* were described earlier. The school probably has some foundation assets or funds to manage, and this is the contribution of the foundation governors. The funds nowadays might be pitifully small: on the other hand they may run into millions. They are usually appointed by the other foundation governors at a meeting of their own. This does not mean that it is a closed shop: anyone is free to contact the clerk to the foundation governors (who might not be the same person as the clerk to the governing body as a whole) to see whether a vacancy exists.
- *Co-opted governors* are elected by the rest of the governing body at a regular meeting. This is how governing bodies make good any deficiencies in their team, by co-opting members of the community, supporters of the school, representatives of religious faiths, money experts, solicitors, business people and others to help them. Some groups represented on the governing body have been known to try to increase their voting power by getting fellow-travellers co-opted.

Governors other than foundation governors usually serve for four years. Teacher governors cease to be a governor as soon as they leave. Parent governors may continue for the four years even if their child has left the school.

WHO CANNOT BE A GOVERNOR?

Stay solvent and out of clink if you want to be a governor. Don't bother to try to become a governor if you are declared bankrupt. The regulations do not permit it. If you agree to settle your debts in full you must wait five years from the date of the bankruptcy agreement before you may become a governor. If the bankruptcy is discharged, you may become a governor again.

The same applies to criminal convictions. If within the previous five years you have been sentenced to at least three months without the option of a fine, you cannot stand as a governor. Moreover, if you have been convicted of 'creating a disturbance on educational premises' as the Local Government (Miscellaneous Provisions) Act of 1982 puts it, you are also disqualified. Curiously, the regulations say that this offence must be 'at the school', so it looks as if you can happily beat up someone at a school where you are not a governor. As a school governor you may well come across those who think that you are committing a nuisance and creating a disturbance merely by *being* on school premises.

Don't think, by the way, if any of the above disasters strike that you can just sit tight and hope that no one will notice. You are required to write to your clerk and confess all – although it has to be said that the regulations do not say what will happen if you don't.

You will also automatically cease to be a governor if you fail to attend meetings for six months without permission or any explanation. Given how busy governors are these days, with numerous sub-committee meetings to attend as well as full governors' meetings, you will not be popular. If your fellow governors, or whoever appointed you, can remember who you are or what you look like, they can re-appoint you. But don't bank on it.

No one under 18 can be a governor. This rules out the practice in some schools in former times of appointing pupil governors, who sometimes talked more sense at meetings than their elders and supposed betters. However governors can, if they wish, pass a resolution admitting pupil *observers*, who may not take part in the meeting or vote. Many have argued that this can be valuable experience for pupils of the workings of democracy, though if the meeting turns out to be more a cure for insomnia than an instructive experience, it may have the opposite effect.

If governors choose to go down that road, however, they must take great care that the vital principles of confidentiality of meetings are not breached. The same care must be exercised if governors decide to go into 'open session' and invite parents or the press. Care must be taken to divide the agenda beforehand into 'unreserved' (public) or 'reserved' (private) business. Another possibility is to have separate meetings: one governing body has 'green' meetings with outsiders (the papers for the meeting are printed on green paper) and normal 'white paper' meetings.

No one can be a governor of more than two maintained schools. This includes both county and voluntary schools. Although the law is not totally clear on the point, it does not seem to apply to governing bodies of grant maintained schools, city technology colleges and independent schools. The older practice of 'grouping' a number of schools under one governing body has now almost entirely disappeared. There is much sense in having governing bodies who concentrate on their own school only, although at times it can be useful to have the governing bodies of two linked schools – say a primary school which feeds its pupils to a nearby secondary school – represented on each other.

Independent schools

The regulations referred to above do not apply to CTCs or independent schools. However, as is the case with all charities, anyone with a financial interest in the school may not be a governor. This has the effect of ruling out teachers as governors because they are paid by the school and parents as governors because they would be voting on fees and other charges. Parliament has seen fit to legislate for this in all types of school except for independent schools and CTCs. Teachers and parents are of course able to attend governors' meetings by specific invitation.

HOW ARE GOVERNING BODIES MADE UP?

The Education Act of 1986 lays this down in considerable detail. In general the bigger the school the bigger the governing body.

LEA and voluntary schools

Schools with fewer than 100 pupils

- 2 parents
- 2 local education authority nominees
- 1 teacher at the school
- the head teacher of the school
- 3 co-opted governors; a voluntary controlled school has 2 foundation governors; and 1 co-opted governor

Schools with 99–299 pupils

- 3 parents
- 3 local education authority nominees
- 1 teacher at the school
- the head teacher of the school
- 5 co-opted governors; a voluntary controlled school has 4 foundation governors and 1 co-opted

Schools with 299–599 pupils

- 4 parents
- 4 local education authority nominees
- 2 teachers at the school
- the head teacher of the school
- 5 co-opted governors; a voluntary controlled school has 4 foundation governors and 1 co-opted governor

Schools with more than 599 pupils

- 5 parents
- 5 local education authority nominees
- 2 teachers at the school
- the head teacher of the school
- 6 co-opted governors; a voluntary controlled school has 4 foundation governors and 2 co-opted governors

There is some subtle thinking in the way these numbers have been put together. For years school governing bodies were dominated – quite legally – by power blocs of local or county councillors. It was argued that only those who had successfully run the gauntlet of election by the public had any real claim to be in authority in schools. Thus parents, members of parent–teacher organisations and others with a real personal interest in the schools were at best a minority – welcome for the most part, but always out-votable. The outcome of this view of how schools should be governed was often that local education authority representatives had no real interest in the school they were governing beyond ensuring that decisions made at County Hall were faithfully and uncritically carried out at school level. Frequently they knew very little about the schools they were appointed to govern and lived a long way from the community served by the school.

Whatever the size of school it can be seen from the figures given above that no single group can dominate a governing body. The parents of pupils at the school elect the parent governors, the teaching staff elects the teacher governors. The biggest single group is the group of co-opted governors and this means that they can wield considerable influence if they are united on an issue. For this reason all the other governors have a real interest in who is co-opted.

Co-opted governors are usually voted onto the governing body at the first meeting of a new governing body, or if and when any resign and must be replaced. All governors should make a real effort to take part in these elections because:

- being the largest single group the co-opted governors have real influence;
- one of the other groups on the governing body might seek to increase its own strength by appointing chums whose support can be relied upon;
- co-opted governors provide an ideal means of bringing onto governing bodies expertise which is not available amongst the other governors. The law requires governing bodies to consider carefully the advantages of having the business community represented. It might also be a good idea to co-opt a member of the *non-teaching staff* of the school: it is sometimes forgotten that they may even outnumber the teaching staff and see the school from a different point of view.

All governors should make it their business to know as much as possible before the election about *all* those who are nominated as co-opted governors. Ghastly mistakes can be made by relying on vague hearsay: 'Oh, yes, I've heard of her. She's supposed to be good. Someone said that the vicar speaks well of her', or – even worse – 'As chair, you can take it from me that Dr Blimenstein is a good sort.' It may well be true, but if you feel that you are being stampeded into too quick an appointment, propose that the matter be deferred to the next meeting – or a special meeting – so that members have time to do their homework thoroughly.

The chair and vice-chair of a governing body are elected at the first meeting of the year, unless the Articles of Government for the school say otherwise. Anyone can be elected to those offices apart from people who work at the school: this bars teachers, the head teacher, the secretary and so on. Nor can a pupil, even if over 18 years old, serve as chair or vice-chair.

As with the election of co-opted governors mentioned above, don't let yourself be stampeded into a quick vote where the chair and vice-chair are concerned. Some well-organised groups may have a caucus meeting beforehand. They then very skilfully propose, second and elect their favourite nominee right at the beginning of a meeting, before other members have had time to draw breath or open their papers. It is surprising how well the old tricks still work. 'Appoint in haste, repent at leisure' is an old saying. Do not vote for someone who could not chair a duet, simply because he might otherwise be upset. Decide whether his slightly injured ego is more important than a year of mayhem for the governors and the school. Chair and vice-chair are key jobs, so choose carefully.

Grant maintained schools

The governing body of a grant maintained school is laid down by the Education Reform Act of 1988 and the Education Act of 1993. It must include

- parent governors
- at least 1, but not more than 2 teacher governors
- the head teacher of the school
- a number of 'first' or 'foundation' governors. If before opting out the school was a county school, these governors are called 'first governors'. If before opting out the school was a voluntary school, they are called 'foundation governors'. Very importantly, the 'first' or 'foundation' governors must outnumber the other governors. Two of them must also be parents of pupils at the school

The Secretary of State can appoint his or her own first governors if the governing body is unable or unwilling to do so. The Secretary of State also has power to appoint up to two additional governors if it seems that in some way the governing body is failing to do what it should. This happened in 1993 when there were much publicised disputes at a school and the Secretary of State appointed a distinguished former Senior Chief Inspector of Schools to the governing body.

Governors of city technology colleges and independent schools

These two types of school are similar in that the law does not prescribe exactly how their governing bodies should be set up or who shall sit on them. Private schools, while certainly independent schools, are to all intents and purposes run as privately-owned businesses and do not have governors as such, although they may have means of consulting parents. Since independent schools and CTCs have no parent local education authority, the governors are responsible for filling their own vacancies and for determining their own size unless these matters are dealt with in their trust deed.

They are however not entirely free agents in this respect. As we have mentioned elsewhere, most independent schools are classified technically as charities, which makes it unlawful for anyone with a financial interest in the school to be a governor. Governors have to decide the school fees to be paid by parents and on staff salaries. Teachers, parents and anyone else paid by the school cannot therefore be governors. There is nothing, however, to prevent a *former* member of staff or a *former* parent from being brought in as a governor.

Readers might then wonder why maintained schools can have teacher governors. The answer is that teachers' salaries are determined nationally, so that school governors' powers are limited to paying them. If governors are given more discretion over teachers' salaries, then this may change. Boarding schools also have a particular problem in that their pupils come from such a wide area – sometimes the other side of the world – that it would be difficult to imagine that a 'representative' parent could be found.

It is very important for all governors to remember that they are *representatives* not *delegates*. Parent governors, like MPs in Parliament, are not obliged to do exactly as their 'electorate' demands. A parent governor must think what is in the best interests of *all* parents and represent that at meetings. The same applies to the elected teacher governors. Moreover any governor can express a view and vote on any issue which comes up.

Everyone is a full governor: there are no first and second class governors (although some governing bodies may sometimes try to create them). It is inadvisable to have section or caucus meetings before governors' meetings to decide what line to pursue. This was something which used to characterise governors' meetings in the 'bad old days': it led to a lack of interest in meetings by other members, to a general feeling of futility and uselessness among many governors, who could have made a much more significant contribution to the life of their school.

WHO ACTUALLY RUNS THE SCHOOL: THE HEAD TEACHER OR THE GOVERNORS?

If the governing body of a school passes a resolution or policy in areas where it has legal powers to do so, the head teacher and staff must follow it. If they refuse, the governing body is entitled to take some form of disciplinary action.

If any reader thinks that governors should adopt this kind of strong-arm tactic as a first rather than last resort, then they should resign and wreak havoc elsewhere. There are a few very important things to remember:

- The head teacher and staff work full-time at the school, five days per week. No matter how dedicated governors are and how much time they devote to their school, the staff will usually know the daily workings of the school better.
- Every day in school hundreds of decisions, major and minor, have to be made. It would simply not be possible to consult the governors over them all.
- The head teacher and the staff are the qualified professionals where pupils are concerned, whereas most governors are lay people.
- The Articles of Government for the school will say that 'the conduct of the school shall be under the direction of the governing body', and that 'the head teacher is responsible for the internal organisation and management of the school and for exercising supervision over the teaching and non-teaching staff (other than the clerk to the governing body)'.

This might sound very much as if governors should always do what the professionals tell them, but this is certainly not the case. For one thing, professional experts of any sort frequently disagree among themselves, as avid watchers of TV courtroom dramas will recognise. Governors frequently have to bring streetwise commonsense to disagreements between head teachers and teacher governors. Governors also have a lot of additional expertise to offer. Parent governors ought to know what parents think of the school; others may know more than the school staff about management, public relations, budgeting, marketing, buildings, finance and so on. The successful governing body accepts that *everybody* has a contribution to make and blends these together. In fact, the governors (and there are some) who think that it is obligatory always to say 'hear, hear' to anything the head teacher says, should also consider their position. Former head teachers or teachers, co-opted for their experience, may be a bit prone to this.

Parliament has decreed that head teachers *must* follow governors' policy on school discipline *where the policy is given in writing*. Governors must also forward to the head teacher for action any resolutions passed at a *quorate* annual governors' meeting with parents. The law also requires the head teacher to act on the outcome of formal appeals to governors, for example about admissions to the school or the exclusion of pupils.

Head teachers are legally required to supply their governors with reports on any aspect of the work of the school. While this can be helpful to governors, it should be used carefully because it can take up a lot of a head teacher's time. Chairs in particular need to be very careful that every single item brought up at a meeting does not lead to a request for a written report from the head teacher.

It has to be said that some head teachers (sometimes for good reasons, sometimes for bad) find it hard to work *with* their governors and seek subtly or crudely to marginalise them. Governors should be on the lookout for a number of traditional strategies in this area. They are usually preventable if attention is drawn to them. Here are a few:

- The head teacher's reports to the governors dwell at length on past glories, like the brilliance of the under-14 girls' netball team in the second half against Gasworks View Comprehensive last year. *Remedy:* Ask about *less* successful performance. While applauding the successes, ask what steps are being taken to improve things in the future.
- The head teacher reports that Mr Clegg has left and a young replacement has been appointed. He thanks the chair for helping make a speedy appointment. *Remedy:* Ask why the governors had not heard in advance that an appointment was to be made. Was it really an emergency? After all, Mr Clegg cannot just quit, he has to give two or three months' notice. How can the governors influence what is taught in the school (it is their legal duty to do so) if they have no say over who is appointed to teach what?
- The head teacher always sits close to the chair at meetings. She and the chair always seem to sing in harmony and are known to spend a lot of time together socially in the interests of working together. The chair refers frequently to avoiding too much work for the governors by constantly calling meetings. The chair refers to what she and the head teacher have done together on your behalf. *Remedy:* Point out that 'chair's action' is now *very* strictly limited by the Education (School Government) Regulations of 1989. If necessary the clerk can show you the appropriate section. You may be called a 'barrack room lawyer' by the head teacher and chair, but if the close collusion is not in the best interests of the school somebody needs to query it. Otherwise you may as well all stay at home and let the dynamic duo get on with it.

THE GOVERNORS' REPORT TO PARENTS AND THE ANNUAL MEETING

Every year the governors must hold an annual meeting with parents at which the governors' report on the school is discussed. Back in 1987 one local authority decreed that all its governing bodies should start their annual report to parents with the following sentence: 'In pursuance of its statutory obligations to parents under Section 30 of the Education (No. 2) Act, 1986, this report details the discharge by the Governing Body of its functions in relation to the School.' If mum and dad, after a hard day's work, pick up a report written like that, it is not surprising that *Coronation Street* wins and the school hall is deserted! The 1986 Act did not intend reports to be a substitute for anaesthetics.

The report must be sent to parents at least two weeks before the meeting. Some features must by law be included:

- The date, time and venue of the meeting.
- The names of members of the governing body together with their period of office. The addresses of the chair and clerk must also appear, so that they can be easily contacted. Telephone numbers are a delicate area.
- Information about the next election of parent governors.
- A summary of the budget for the previous year, stating how money was spent.
- Information about unauthorised absence of pupils (better known as 'truancy tables'). Until the DFE tidies up its procedure for collecting data and defines precisely what it means by 'truancy', these tables are likely to be meaningless, and certainly not a basis for comparing your school with any other. Ask your head for more details about this.
- Examination results (A level, GCSE and National Curriculum tests).
- How the school is strengthening its links with the community and the police.
- Details of any changes to the school's brochure or prospectus since the last meeting.
- A report on the discussion about seeking grant maintained status, a debate which must take place annually.

It cannot be said that attendance at these meetings has really gripped parents' imagination (apart from meetings specifically devoted to opting out which have on occasion been stormy), although the idea is fundamentally good. There is nothing in the regulations to say that the report cannot be written in a lighthearted, friendly way. Above all the report should look good, and not look like a cross between junk mail and a council tax demand. The language can be informal, although it must be *accurate*: if it isn't, expect a parent or two to score points at the meeting. The report is meant to involve parents in the life of the school and make them feel that you really *do* care about their views. There is nothing worse than a world-weary chair of governors opening a meeting with a 'I hope this won't take too long' speech. It is a parents' meeting, not a dental appointment. Skilful governors relegate all the dry statistical stuff to the back page (shrinking it until it's just still legible) and fill the agenda with more vital items such as:

- The school wants to make pupils study more technology. What do you think?

- The school meals are ghastly. What can we do about it?
- If we started school at 8.45 and finished at 4.15 we could start to teach a lot of additional subjects. What do you think?
- Should teachers move up with their classes?
- Here are some new developments (for example, a foreign language in the primary school, a humanities course, improving our special educational needs provision, outdoor education and educational trips), so what do you think about them?

Schools frequently have facilities for desktop publishing (if they don't, parents may have access). One idea might be to publish the report as a tabloid newspaper. Older children could do a good job here. Diagrams, pie-charts, and children's drawings are all eye-catching and attractive. Perhaps a class could describe what it has achieved during the year. A governor could be persuaded to write about life (or death) as a governor. The meeting is a good way for governors to catch the mood of parents and to pick up any good ideas around. Parents must be told:

- That they can raise issues and have them discussed. They should not take up any *individual* grievances: these must be dealt with by the head teacher as usual.
- What has happened about any resolutions passed at last year's parents' meeting. There may be very good practical reasons why all of year nine could not visit a coal mine or study basket-weaving, but you must explain them. You may be sent back again to reconsider, however.
- That they can reach the governors by writing or phoning.

Some governing bodies may need to be reminded that we are talking here about a *governors'* report to parents, not a head teacher's report. The head teacher should certainly be asked to provide information, but what is not needed is a rehash of the same head teacher's report to parents, which they will have already heard. Some head teachers feel pressured by their governors to write the report, which is not appropriate.

Chapter 2

Governors' responsibilities

They say that if the guards on trains insisted on carrying out all their responsibilities each time a train pulled into a station, such as checking the wheels, balancing the load equally across all carriages and so on, no train would ever run. The same probably applies to governors. Fortunately no individual governor or governing body is expected to live in the school every day: that is what the head teacher and staff are there for. So don't resign your governorship just yet.

In this chapter we look at some of the responsibilities which governors carry nowadays. No one governor, even the chair, is expected to be an expert on all of them. Governing bodies usually set up a system of sub-committees, each of which has a particular responsibility such as curriculum or staffing or buildings and premises. There are many other possibilities, and governors usually choose to sit on the sub-committee which interests them most. Some governors like to sit on a different sub-committee every year so that in time they get a broad overview. Although governing bodies rely very heavily on the wisdom of their sub-committees, because they have studied matters of concern to them very closely, they are not *obliged* always to take their advice. It is only the *full* governing body which makes decisions about the school, not its sub-committees or individuals, so you are not empowered to storm into a classroom and fire Mr Scroggins.

GETTING TO KNOW ABOUT GOVERNORS' WORK

There is nothing quite like learning on the job. However, it is wise to make sure that you at least know about the various 'bibles' of the business and can lay your hands on them as soon as the need arises and before anything goes wrong. We have included a select bibliography of relevant reading at the end of this book.

It is also worthwhile keeping up with what is happening in the field of education, which seems to change just as soon as you think you have caught up with it. Weekly education papers such as *The Times Educational Supplement* or *Education* are very good value. There are now local and national confederations of governors you can join, as well as various regular journals or newsletters for governors: your governing body should perhaps buy copies of the best of these and circulate them. Let us start by looking at a few key aspects of being a governor.

The Instrument and Articles of Government

The Instrument of Government says, among other things, how the governing body is to be made up and who nominates or elects governors. The Articles of Government explain what the governors of the school are to do. Every school has such documents. At one time it was these documents which controlled governors' work in all but independent schools, and they could vary from area to area in the country. Nowadays they have been largely superseded by national legislation and regulations. However it is essential to know what they say because they may give you additional powers and duties. The Articles cannot of course go against national policy.

LOCAL MANAGEMENT OF SCHOOLS

The term 'local financial management' was brought into use by the Education Reform Act of 1988. Very rapidly it was realised that what was intended was 'local management of schools' and the term was changed to the latter. Its implementation has been the biggest single revolution in the management of schools for many years. Prior to 1988 the most important financial decisions about schools were made at County Hall by local education authorities. They paid staff and looked after the buildings: the governors' job was really to give advice to the LEA. All this has changed with local financial management.

Delegated budgets

In a nutshell, governors are given a sum of money every year and have to run the school with it. Before you run out shouting, 'Money! We're rich! Power! At last!', the bad news is that responsibility for money is quite an exacting assignment, especially if there doesn't seem to be enough of it. If yours is a school which comes under an LEA, the money comes from them. If yours is a grant maintained school (an 'opted out' school), or a city technology college, it comes from Whitehall. There is always speculation about who gets the best financial deal and whether one should try to change status to get it.

If you are a governor of an independent school you will be constantly concerned that sufficient parents will be able and willing to pay the fees you have previously set. If they aren't, you may well go broke. Other schools could in theory go broke too, but the Education Reform Act gives local education authorities the power to take back control of a school's budget if

"GOVERNORS ARE RESPONSIBLE FOR SCHOOL BUDGETS"

it seems that the governors are heading for financial disaster. Independent schools are on their own.

Local education authorities first decide how much money overall they are going to spend on schools in the following year, starting in April: this is the GSB (general schools' budget). Next they keep back the funds they need to run their school meals service, if they have decided to keep one, to provide transport to schools for pupils who are entitled to it, and for bigger items such as capital spending on school buildings.

Local authorities must then distribute the vast majority of what is left to their schools, in accordance with a local formula which is agreed with the Department for Education in London. This takes into account such things as the state and age of your buildings, an allowance for small schools, any peculiar problems your school may have and anything else you can wangle under the formula. Every year there are grumbles about the formula and whether it applies fairly to your school. That said, most governors would prefer this to the previous system by which one had to stand in the queue and ask for money, never knowing even if there was any.

Most of the funding for each school is calculated from the number of pupils in the school. This – as was intended – can lead to schools competing with each other for additional pupils by trying to become more attractive and popular. Certainly it brings in more money. On the other hand an increase in pupil numbers can actually *increase expenditure*, because extra teaching staff may be needed if some classes become too large and have to be divided. Governors need to calculate very carefully here. The size of the classes in which their children are taught is often of great concern to parents, particularly in independent schools where parents believe that small classes are worth the financial outlay and often sacrifice.

The formulae also give money specifically for pupils classified as having special educational needs. This term came into being after the Education Act of 1981 which sought to look after those pupils with learning difficulties of many sorts, usually slow learners. Dyslexia and other reading difficulties are another example. Staffing costs are usually high in these cases, as more individual attention is needed. Schools which make top level provision for their slow learners usually feel strongly that the element for this in their budget is far too low, and there is a temptation – which most governing bodies to their credit resist – to try to avoid admitting such pupils. The Education Act of 1993 has plugged this gap by giving local education authorities in difficult cases the power to make governors admit pupils.

One irritation for governors – although it is difficult to see how it could be otherwise – is that the annual budget share for each school has to be calculated in advance on the *estimated* numbers in the school for the following year. Governors obviously need to know how much they will be receiving as soon as possible before the financial year starts in April. Local education authorities are required to tell schools in March, which means that they must start calculating several months before. Pressures from parents to admit pupils, as well as the outcomes of school admissions appeals, can mean that schools find themselves with more pupils than the numbers from which their annual grant was calculated. Only sometimes can things be put right at that stage.

Governors generally can choose whether to have the budget money (apart from the money for salaries which is kept back by the LEA and paid directly to staff) paid into their school's bank or building society account, or whether to let their LEA do the book-keeping, accounting and annual auditing (but not of course make detailed decisions about what to spend, because only the governors can do that).

Governors who choose to have the money in a bank or building society account, in common with the governors of grant maintained, independent and city technology colleges, have to set these things up for themselves – hence the attraction of getting an accountant, a finance expert or a retired bank manager co-opted as a governor. The benefit of schools doing this for themselves is that they have their own cheque book and can pay bills promptly and perhaps in that way get a cash discount. Governors often say that it makes them feel very much 'in charge'.

Other school income

Schools are also free to raise additional income in any other (legal!) way they wish. Fund-raising by parent–teacher associations is already well known, and nowadays governors often look at what their school might earn by so-called 'lettings' – hiring out whatever facilities they can. Really enterprising schools have been able to get sponsorship from local and national firms for computer rooms, word-processing facilities, additional buildings and a whole host of other items of expenditure. Money can also come in from school concerts and plays. Governors are asking themselves whether the school hall might be let for all sorts of community activities, not forgetting of course to include the costs of any damage and cleaning up afterwards in the letting charges. Swimming pools and sporting facilities are another distinct possibility, although governors need to take care that their enthusiasm for money-raising doesn't get in the way of the use of school facilities by their own pupils. Overuse of football pitches can easily mean that school matches have to be cancelled, which is clearly counter-productive. Some crafty governors of secondary schools are keen to encourage pupils from local primary schools to use their splendid facilities with a view to encouraging them to choose their school when they transfer!

The school fund

Schools have always had a fund with such a name or similar. Into this go all bits and pieces of money which come into the school, but *not* the budget funds from the LEA or the Department for Education in the case of grant maintained schools or CTC. Bring and buy sales and raffles, as well as the school tuck shop if you run one, can produce income and there can be special accounts where money for school journeys, plays and concerts is held temporarily. It is worthwhile to find out about value added tax, in case the school has to pay or claim back VAT. Local authorities usually have guidelines about how school funds and gifts are to be handled (but not spent; that is for the school to decide). These are intended to protect the funds against fraud or other corruption. Schools, by the way, are not allowed to borrow money, so that they do not have any savings or investments. The exceptions to this are independent schools and those schools which are supported in part by trusts or endowments from the past.

Voluntary contributions

Some schools have found that some of their parents are willing to make voluntary payments to their children's schools to pay for a few extra items for the school. Governors need to be very careful indeed here. Education must by law be provided *free*, apart from some carefully defined exceptions, and any attempt to compel parents to pay would be illegal.

Charges to parents

The borderline between what is provided free in education (i.e. by the taxpayer) and what is paid for directly by parents, has always been blurred. Parents buy games and PE kit and provide materials for activities such as cookery: they also often buy musical instruments. In many countries of continental Europe they have to buy school textbooks. The borderline also shifts from time to time.

The position since 1988 is that:

- no charge may be made for education during school hours;
- no charge may be made for any course in school leading to a public examination (such as GCSE), nor for entry fees for the examinations, nor for any transport in connection with such courses;

but

- a charge may be made for individual instrumental tuition or for tuition in groups of four and fewer;
- a charge may be made for overnight accommodation on a residential trip;
- a charge may be made for an educational activity which falls mainly (50 per cent) out of school hours;
- a charge may be made to the parent to recover any examination entry fee if the pupil fails without good reason to meet any examination requirement;
- a charge may be made to cover the entry costs for any public examination beyond those the pupil would normally take at school;
- a charge may be made of the full cost of any optional extra.

So here is one particularly sensitive matter. The governing body has to decide, in the light of all the circumstances, whether in fact to charge for these things and how much.

Now the good news . . .

If you are beginning to wonder whether, as an amateur, you could easily wind up in jail by making a mess of all these financial matters, be reassured. The

1988 Education Reform Act accepts that with the best will in the world school financial controls might go wrong. If they do, you will not be held liable. Your local authority can also take control of your budget – it makes you look a failure, but that's better than six months in jug. It is worth remembering that governors of local authority, voluntary and grant maintained schools and CTCs are nowadays carrying no more responsibility than the governors of independent schools have carried literally for centuries. However, *'with the best will in the world'* is very important. If you and your fellow governors decide to blow the lot on an evening's pub-crawl, the consequences could be very nasty indeed.

... and a warning

Governors quite understandably are often wary and apprehensive about financial management. Some, particularly in smaller schools, have been known to try to leave the whole business to their head teacher. However, in law the budget is the governors' responsibility and no one else's; moreover the head teacher may know little more than the governors about financial matters. In any case, are you paying the head to be an accountant and book-keeper or the head teacher of your school? If things go wrong, the governors will not be able to hide behind their head teacher.

Bigger schools might be attracted by the idea of having a bursar, as most independent schools do. Remember, though, that money spent on his or her services is money you must take every year from some other part of the school's finances. It also seems a little odd to have to ask a bursar for money, when governors at one time objected to having to ask their LEA.

Drawing up school budgets

This can seem frightening to governors who are non-professionals but it is in general straightforward. In the case of local authority schools procedural guidelines will be laid down. Towards the end of the financial year the head teacher will draw up a draft budget for the school for the coming year. In some circumstances governors' sub-committees, of which the head teacher is also a member, may also draw up budgets for the areas which concern them – governors may for example have a catering scheme in their school. At that stage a small sub-committee (probably the governors' finance sub-committee) will try to fit all the draft budgets together in a sensible way. This meeting can be fraught, since it nearly always results in scuppering someone's cherished plan. When the overall draft budget is complete, it goes to the full governing body for approval.

The governing body cannot approve the budget of course until it knows for sure just how much money will be forthcoming. Although the budget formulae mentioned above are supposed to be simple to understand so that schools can make a very close estimate of what they will receive, in practice the estimates can be significantly wrong. Governors then have to do a great deal of moving money around and, sad to say, cutting or even slashing some budgets.

During the year money can be moved around from budget to budget – this is known as virement. If there is a sudden outbreak of flu or other reasons for staff absences, temporary ('supply') teachers will have to be brought in. Although governors usually budget for this, it is easy not to have enough. Then the head teacher and staffing sub-committee may recommend a replacement teacher who is on a very high salary, perhaps much more than his or her predecessor. You will then have to raid someone else's budget – not the sure way to win friends.

Perhaps the most intractable problem in school finance is that teachers' and other salaries and wages usually make up 80 per cent or so of a school's expenditure because teaching is a labour-intensive business. For this reason the salaries and wages budget must always come under close scrutiny: far-sighted governors will look to the possibilities in future of computer-assisted learning and more training of pupils in study skills as ways of containing salary costs and improving the learning resources in their school. There is much to be said for the view that such developments are educationally desirable in their own right, given the world in which our children will work.

What is the money spent on?

The major headings are shown below, but not in any particular order since this will vary from school to school.

- *Staffing.* As we have already mentioned, this is always the biggest item of expenditure. It includes caretaking, cleaning, secretarial, maintenance and administrative staff, as well as teaching staff. Don't forget your budget for supply teachers. Like the rest of us, teachers have to have time off for good reason.
- *Building maintenance.* Governors with well-built and newish schools are lucky here.
- *Decoration.* Graffiti and vandalism drive governors wild nowadays.
- *All sorts of cleaning materials.* It's surprising how these costs can run away if not tightly controlled. Repairs to the hall floor after somebody's annual shindig?
- *Heating and other fuel costs.* It may be worthwhile to pay for a professional survey to see whether you are wasting money.
- *Fees for public examinations, like GCSE and A level in secondary schools.* Some are cheaper than others. There is often a small-scale 'price war' going on between the Examining Boards, who are in competition with each other for customers. But before you dash in to make a quick saving, beware

teachers' passionate devotion to the examination syllabuses which they know best and can teach best.

- *Teaching materials*. This includes textbooks, paper, and equipment such as computers, overhead projectors and equipment for science teaching. Paper usage in schools is very difficult to control and science teaching is expensive.
- *Pupil support costs*. An LEA may well include money for some pupils' uniform clothing and footwear in your budget. There will be no virement for this. It must be spent on these items only.
- *Furniture costs for staff and pupils*. They can't sit on the floor all day.
- *Office costs*. Most schools now are computerised for routine administration. Watch out for photocopying costs. There has been much media coverage about these and the best way of reducing them. Watch out for teaching staff who use the office photocopier for classwork, but do not charge it to the teaching budget.
- *Various bits of technology*. This might include security alarms, emergency lighting, 'clocking in and out' systems for pupils instead of the traditional marking of the register and, nowadays, 'smart cards' for pupils to pay for their school meals.
- *Teacher training courses*. Often referred to as 'INSET' (in-service education and training), or 'professional development', this is the professional lifeblood of teachers, particularly where courses or examination syllabuses are changing, as the National Curriculum may. It is just as necessary, perhaps even more so, in schools where staff rarely change, so that new ideas are hard to get. Remember that if our doctors did not go on courses to keep up to date, many of us would now be dead.

Grant maintained, independent school and CTC governors also need to plan their capital spending well in advance. For all other schools the responsibility for this lies with the local authority.

Putting services out to tender

Governors are generally required to put the supply of equipment and services out to competitive tender. The most common candidates are cleaning and catering. Your local authority, if you have one, will no doubt offer to continue to supply these services, but you should look at what is offered and at what price.

This can be a disastrously tricky area for the unwary. As a general principle *read the small print* of the agreement before you sign it. The cheapest might not be exactly what you need and later alterations can be very expensive. Photocopiers can run away with your funds if the price per copy in the lease is extortionate. You may find that your good value outside caterer will charge the earth if you later decide that you want tea and buns for the PTA, the staff cricket match – or even the governors. How often do you want the playing fields mowed? More often in good growing weather? Who is to pay for the ground staff's *equipment* – you or the contractor? Every one a gem and rife for conflict.

A good local authority ought to know just what its schools want, and should therefore put in an attractive offer. Don't however assume that it is bound to be the best. Competition is keen and commercial suppliers are fast learning the ropes. A governor with a knowledge of tendering can be worth his or her weight in gold.

Books and educational equipment

This may well be the biggest item of expenditure after salaries. Money can be saved in considerable amounts by shopping around for paper, computers, television sets, tape recorders. It might also make sense to go in for consortium buying with other schools in the neighbourhood – if nothing else this reduces delivery costs, which can be considerable.

SCHOOL DEVELOPMENT PLANS

Forward planning is not just a financial matter. Schools need a development plan so that people can see where they are going. It makes no sense for governors to live hand to mouth, living from crisis to crisis until one day some disaster occurs about which they can do nothing. If the numbers of pupils in your school are set to rise, you ought to forecast this well in advance, so that you can be sure that money will be available to increase staff numbers and provide extra furniture. Perhaps you will need extra accommodation as well.

If the numbers in the early years of your school are large, it is reasonable to expect larger numbers in your upper junior or sixth form classes in a few years' time. If you wish to change the curriculum in your school (teach Russian instead of German, for example), the best time to do this will be when a suitable staff vacancy occurs. You are probably not in a position to say *when* that will happen, but you can lay plans for when it does.

All this means that schools need to draw up development plans for the future so as not to be caught napping. A 1989 publication from the Department for Education entitled 'Planning for School Development' lists the advantages of having a development plan:

1 It focuses attention on the aims of education, especially the learning and achievement, broadly defined, of all pupils.
2 It provides a comprehensive and co-ordinated approach to *all* aspects of planning, one which covers curriculum and assessment, teaching management and organisation, finance and resources.
3 It captures the long-term vision for the school within which manageable

short-term goals are set. The priorities contained in the plan represent the school's translation of policy into its agenda for action.

4 It helps to relieve the pressure on teachers caused by the pace of change. Teachers come to exercise greater control over change rather than feeling controlled by it.

5 The achievements of teachers in promoting innovation and change receive wider recognition, so that their confidence rises.

6 The quality of staff development improves. In-service training and ap-praisal help the school to work more effectively and teachers to acquire new knowledge and skills as part of their professional development.

7 The partnership between the teaching staff and governing body is strengthened.

8 The task of reporting on the work of the school is made easier.

In essence the activity of drawing up a development plan requires governors to find out the answers to the following questions:

- Where is the school now?
- What changes do we need to make?
- How shall we manage these changes over time?
- How shall we know whether our management of these changes has been successful?

MARKETING THE SCHOOL

Anyone who runs a course nowadays entitled 'How to market your school' or 'Selling your school' (not literally!) is guaranteed several rooms full of teachers and governors wanting to know how. The driving force is that the more pupils you have, the more money your school attracts, whether yours is an independent school, a grant maintained one or whatever. Here are some other reasons why a marketing strategy is a good idea:

- Good news for one school is good for all. The media are obsessed with failure in schools – you have to broadcast your own *successes*. There may be many.
- Schools are increasingly creative in recruiting pupils. Rest on your laurels and you could find numbers dwindle.
- The effects of legislation widening parents' choice of school are still growing, even years after the legislation was enacted.
- It is sometimes necessary to correct or counteract poor publicity
- It can be a real morale-booster for staff and pupils to receive good publicity

Governors, usually working with the school staff, often start with a SWOT analysis – an analysis of strengths, weaknesses, opportunities and threats. This can be a very useful exercise in getting to know your school: the whole governing body can take part with groups looking at each heading and then putting their contributions together.

Strengths

List the *good* things about your school. Technology? Performing arts? Modern languages? Sports? Don't confuse these with good examination results. Many children really enjoy some areas of their work and flock to it, even if they are not especially good at it. Music is a good example.

Weaknesses

You have to be candid here. If you have problems with discipline and a poor school record in examinations, there is no choice but to get together with the head teacher and decide what you are going to do. You might not get it right the first time, but ignoring it or, worse, being timid about it does not help.

Opportunities

When and where can you publicise your school? Tee-shirts or uniform? Has the school a press officer who will tell the local papers what is going on in the school, about pupils' achievements, visits, links with the community or industry, your new classes in Italian (open to parents)? Has the press ever published a profile of your head teacher, or other characters in the school? Pupils from one school set up experiments in science and technology in a shopping centre and invited shoppers to take part. Regular 'Open Days' supported by advertising aimed at prospective parents are effective. When thinking about using opportunities to the best advantage, consider these two points:

1 *Where do people meet?* Libraries, waiting rooms, queues, outside the school, pubs, hairdressers, groups who meet in your school, evening classes.
2 *Who else will be interested?* Community centres, local firms (personnel departments know of employees moving into the area), voluntary organisations, welfare agencies.

Threats

A variety of factors can threaten what the school is doing. People may be moving out of the neighbourhood, particularly if it is changing its purpose and becoming industrial and commercial, rather than residential. Several staff may be coming up for retirement, with all that expertise and commitment flowing away one day.

Other schools might pose a threat, particularly if they become aggressive in their recruiting. Have a good look at what they are doing (they may be looking at you!). Collect their brochures to see what is happening. Find out what parents like about them. Are they laying on transport to enable children to reach them? Will it make a difference if they 'opt out'? What sort of impression does *your* school make on first-time visitors? Are they given somewhere comfortable to sit and something to read while waiting? Toilet facilities? Efficient and *friendly* sign-posting, or 'NO ADMITTANCE UNLESS ON BUSINESS' or 'WAIT HERE UNTIL COLLECTED BY MEMBER OF STAFF'?

On the other hand, do not overplay the idea of 'beating the opposition'. Collaboration between schools can be very healthy and desirable for the neighbourhood. If schools only try to do each other down, nobody wins and the local atmosphere becomes sour.

COMMUNICATIONS ABOUT YOUR SCHOOL

These include letters to parents, brochures, school posters and newsletters. Here are a few important considerations:

- Do you have a notepaper heading which everyone recognises immediately as yours? Does your school have a distinctive colour which is recognised as yours?
- Are your letters always well typed and presented? If necessary, pay for your secretary to go on a course.
- Spelling and punctuation errors *never* help the image of a *school*.
- Is it always made clear that parents and children are welcome to visit?
- Is your brochure, or leaflet, written in simple language and easy to read?
- Does it have a clear map?
- The most important things about schools are children, teachers and atmosphere. Is your publicity more like a Roll of Honour combined with a house agent's leaflet?
- Can *children* read and understand your publicity? Some children have a lot of influence in choosing the school they go to.
- Does it say clearly what interested parents and children should do next?

GOVERNORS' SUB-COMMITTEES: OFFICIAL AND UNOFFICIAL

Governing bodies need to set up sub-committees to share out the work. Each sub-committee specialises in a particular area of business. Governing bodies can have as many sub-committees as they like. Each sub-committee can appoint its own chair and, if it wishes, invite non-governors to serve for their specialist knowledge. What you do in your school will depend on its size, complexity, and the way members want to conduct the business. What suits a small primary school may not fit neatly with the needs of a large secondary school. Amongst possible sub-committees are:

- *Property sub-committee* This will make recommendations about decorating, furnishings, the playing fields, the swimming pool if there is one and probably also lettings of any part of the premises.

- *Finance and General Purposes sub-committee* This will keep an eye on how the budget is being spent after it has been agreed by the full governing body. It may have authority to move money from one budget heading to another.
- *Curriculum and Staffing sub-committee* It is important to keep these two aspects together. Some schools give 'staffing' to the Finance sub-committee, because it is so expensive, but that means that the curriculum has to be planned without reference to the teachers who are going to teach it.

Sub-committees meet as the need arises, sometimes very often, especially if there is a pressing problem. The clerk to the governors will usually organise a round of meetings and the last one will be the meeting of the full governing body which will consider all the recommendations from its sub-committees.

Other sub-committees are created and meet as the need arises, which might only be once a year, or on a special occasion, or to deal with an emergency. For example:

- *Appeals sub-committees.* These will deal with appeals by parents when their child has been refused admission to the school or excluded for poor behaviour.
- *Disciplinary sub-committee.* This might have to be set up to meet a particular crisis on a disciplinary matter to do with the staff, perhaps an appeal against dismissal.
- *A Marketing or Promotion sub-committee.* This may be a good idea, in certain circumstances.

A good introduction for new governors is to join a sub-committee as soon as possible and start to concentrate on one aspect of the life of the school. It helps, too, if governors move from one sub-committee to another over a period of time, as a way of ensuring that possible future chairs and vice-chairs have 'been around a bit'.

One very important thing to remember about any sub-committee to do with *appeals* is that it must not in fairness contain governors who have been involved with earlier decisions. It must be seen to approach the matter with a fresh mind. If the staffing sub-committee for example has recommended the dismissal of a member of staff and this has been confirmed by the full governing body, no one involved in those earlier discussions or decisions can hear an appeal. If you fail to observe this (and finding enough people can sometimes be very difficult for smaller governing bodies), the law will slap your hand and you will get your problem teacher back with a grin on his or her face, and possibly a large cheque for compensation, something which would not go down too well in the staffroom.

One characteristic of school governing bodies is that they have been known to develop *unofficial* sub-committees. A chair, for example, will consult one or two close governor colleagues about a matter and tell the next meeting what has been decided and even acted upon. The excuse will be 'pressure of time' dressed up in some way. It might even be 'I didn't think that you'd all want to be bothered with it or come to a meeting', or 'It had to be done quickly', or 'Since most of you are new, we felt [note the 'we': a new committee has come into being] that you wouldn't yet know enough to be able to help.'

These things can happen in all innocence. Such groups may consist of the longest-serving governors, by now old friends. Sometimes foundation governors meeting as a group see themselves as an all-powerful inner cabinet of the school. Sometimes also, sad to say, 'chair's pals' are the creation of egocentric chairs who think that they alone know what is best for their school and dislike governors' meetings where colleagues actually argue with them. Worst of all in this respect is the creation, often when a governors' meeting is not really awake to what is happening, of an 'Executive' sub-committee, or 'Chairperson's group'. Any such group rapidly takes to itself any governors' business it chooses. After a short while the other governors will simply stop coming to meetings. Why waste the time? *They* have sorted it all out anyway. Joan Sallis refers to this as 'A and B team governors'.

It is helpful to governors blighted by such unfortunate practices to know that they are banned by the Education (School Government) Regulations of 1989. The chair or, in his or her absence, the vice-chair can act alone *only* if a delay 'would be likely to be seriously detrimental [note the word *seriously*] to the interests of the school, or to the interests of any registered pupil at the school, his parent, or a person employed at the school'. A delay is defined as: 'a day extending beyond the day preceding the earliest date on which it would reasonably be practicable for a meeting of the governing body to be held'. All governors should remember this, and demand to know the reasons, if confronted by over-enthusiastic 'chair's action'.

Similarly, the 'constitution, membership and proceedings of any such committee shall be determined by the governing body'. In practice this means that the governing body as a whole should decide what sub-committees to set up and why, how long they are to remain in existence and, very importantly, decide what the limits of their responsibility are. Any unofficial sub-committee has no standing whatsoever.

Delegation to sub-committees

It is the governing body *as a whole* which in law is responsible for running the school, not individuals or sub-committees. Sub-committees usually may only make recommendations to the full governing body. However common sense tells us that, in a big school, to bring twenty or so governors together for meetings every time a decision is needed would rapidly produce fatigue, and may indeed be impossible because governors have many other good things to do. Permitting sub-committees which are much smaller and easier to bring together to take *some* final decisions and act upon them is a sensible thing to do.

That said, however, the Regulations mentioned above are very strict about what the full governing body may *not* delegate to individuals or a sub-committee, and must be decided by the full governing body. These matters can of course be *discussed* first by a sub-committee. It is quite a long list and space prevents us from giving readers more than a general idea of what they are:

- changing the character of a school, or closing it
- policy on school admissions
- approval of school premises
- appointment of governors
- matters to do with the curriculum
- school hours, terms and holidays
- discipline policy
- approving the governors' annual report to parents
- control of political indoctrination
- policy on sex education
- policy on collective worship and religious education
- provision of information to parents
- decisions about seeking grant maintained status
- policies on charges and remissions
- appointment of a head teacher or deputy head teacher
- appointment of chair or vice-chair
- dates of governors' meetings; any three governors can call one
- whether any matter may be delegated to a sub-committee or an individual

Governor readers are recommended to consult the full regulations and not to assume that their chair or clerk has already done so. It can be very difficult if decisions made in good faith but in ignorance are later declared invalid and matters have to be reopened.

GOVERNORS' MEETINGS

We deal with the actual workings of governors' meetings more fully in Chapter 4, but here are some important constitutional matters. The Education (School Government) Regulations of 1989 have a lot to say about these.

- *Full meetings* of the governing body must be held at least once in every school term. Sub-committees can meet as often as they need to. The clerk to the governors calls meetings on the agreed dates by sending out the agendas and other papers in advance.
- *Any three governors can ask for a meeting to be called* and the clerk when

asked must do so. Beware of the trio of governors who keep calling meetings at awkward times to suit themselves. Soon they have effectively taken over the management of your school.

- *The quorum* for termly governors' meetings is one-third of the members, rounded up to a whole number. Your Articles of Government may decree a larger number, but this may not be greater than two-fifths. There is an important exception to the rule about one-third of governors having to be present for routine meetings, however. If the governors' meeting wants to co-opt other governors, the quorum goes up to three-quarters, rounded up to a whole number. This again emphasises the need for all governors to turn up for the first meeting of the year. The three-quarters quorum also applies in the very special case where the governors of a *local authority* boarding school meet to appoint a parent governor: elections in such a case would be difficult because by and large parents of children in a boarding school know each other less well.
- *If the annual parents' meeting wishes to pass formal and binding resolutions*, the number of parents present must equal 20 per cent of the pupils in the school.
- *Withdrawal from meetings* may be required from time to time. As is customary in local and national government, governors who are likely to profit financially from anything being discussed at meetings *must* leave the room while that item is being discussed. They certainly should not take part in discussion or vote on it. This applies to governors' spouses and relatives living with them. The person concerned simply says 'I declare an interest', and then leaves the meeting until the item is over. The chair may have to remind members of this requirement, especially if some crafty entrepreneur is trying to sit there looking innocent.

The principle of being an interested party is not solely financial, and is largely a matter of commonsense. If your spouse or partner with whom you are living is up for a job of any sort at the school, or is liable to be transferred, sacked or promoted, or your own child is up before the governors for some disciplinary offence, then obviously you cannot take part in that meeting – nor can you if the matter under discussion is whether to admit your own child to the school. You must also leave, even if you are the clerk, if the subject under discussion is the possibility of some disciplinary action against you.

As we have noted above, it follows in the interests of impartial justice that you cannot be a member of an appeal panel involving some action which you yourself started. For example, if you see Wayne, Shane and Duane creating mayhem behind the bike shed, report them to the head teacher and the head teacher takes action before the governors, you must withdraw from that meeting – although of course the governors may call you as a witness. In such cases the head teacher also can only act as a witness, not as a governor. The point is that the governors hearing the case must be seen to be unbiased.

The list of reasons for withdrawal is not exhaustive, and your articles of government may add some. For example it may be necessary in your school to ask a teacher governor to leave the room if what is being discussed is the appointment, dismissal, promotion or disciplinary affairs of a member of staff who is senior to the teacher governor.

The head teacher's report

This is a major agenda item at any full governors' meeting. It can be interesting, exciting even, or it can be a potent sleeping pill with no side effects. It may dominate what governors talk about for the rest of the meeting. For that reason it could, at its worst, enable one governor, the head teacher, to control the whole meeting. The head teacher and the governors *jointly* carry *full* responsibility for the school. It follows therefore that the governors will want to know about how their policies for the school are being implemented and how budgets are being spent. They will also want to know of anything which is likely to need the involvement of the governors.

There are no regulations covering the way in which any head teacher's report should be presented: it is for the head and governors to agree on what is best. It is probably a good idea to agree on a number of headings to guide the production of each report. We give a few ideas below.

1 The management of the school
   * Is the school following the development plan?
   * How are the pupils progressing?
   * Has the curriculum changed in any way?
   * How is the head teacher monitoring changes?
   * Are the buildings being well maintained?
   * Are the budgets on target?
   * Have there been any staff changes?
2 The future
   * Are there any difficulties ahead?
   * Which areas of the school's work are coming up for review?
   * What capital or equipment expenditure is going to be needed?
   * Are there likely to be any staff changes?
   * If so, how is it suggested that they be filled?
   * Is a school inspection due, and if so, what needs to be done in preparation?
3 What advice is needed?
4 What decisions are needed?

Above all, the report needs to be forward looking and not dwell too long on the past. This is the only way in which governors can be fully involved.

Representing those who selected you

Obviously you will feel a degree of loyalty towards the group that made you a governor, be it the staff of the school, the parents or the local authority. However once you are a governor you are there in your own right and not a delegate. This means that you are free to act, think and vote as you see fit *on any issue* in the interests of your school, even if on occasion this may run counter to the interests of the group which put you there. In practice this issue arises most frequently in the case of parent governors, where you may have to represent as many as 2000+ parents in a big comprehensive school. Parent governors can find themselves pressurised by articulate groups of parents with a particular view of what should happen, or even be lobbied by opposing groups. The task of parent governors is to speak up for parents as a whole group, not for only a few of them.

Finally, if you are ever obliged not to support your own group's views at governors' meetings, do not let threats of being 'unseated' cause you to break the rules about confidentiality. If you do, you risk alienating your group, your fellow governors and quite possibly the LEA as well.

Confidentiality

Governors are in a privileged position and often come into possession of information which in the best interests of all should remain confidential. You may be called upon, for example, to review the case of a 14-year-old at your school who has just given birth. To talk about the case around your community would be a grave breach of trust.

Although commonsense suggests that matters such as the above should remain confidential, in fact *everything* discussed at governors' meetings should be regarded as confidential. It is the *published minutes* which tell the outside world what has happened, and nothing else. There are good reasons for this. One is that no one would feel free to speak openly if they thought that everything they said was going to be bandied around the supermarket or appear in the press. Sometimes too a decision taken by the governors in good faith turns out to be inappropriate when further information comes to light and obliges them to change their mind. Beware too of discussing publicly allegations that may have been made. Slander and libel laws are very strong in the UK.

Because of this confidentiality you are given what the law calls 'qualified privilege'. Like MPs in the Commons you can speak freely and say exactly what you like without fear of legal action. But this privilege covers you only during formal governors' meetings and does not cover you if you speak maliciously. And you must watch what you say if your meeting is held publicly, for example at the annual governors' meeting with parents.

You may perhaps feel that this system is set up to gag you. This is a false impression. The minutes of governors' meetings must be published and made available at the school to anyone who wishes to see them. This is the official means of communication. It is not for individual governors to decide what is or what is not confidential, since opinions will differ and chaos will ensue.

SCHOOL STAFF

Nowadays governors appoint and dismiss staff. We shall deal with the important matter of staff appointments in Chapter 3. Staff in LEA schools are in a unique position: they have a contract of employment not with the governors as in voluntary and other types of school, but with the authority. The authority must however act on governors' requests to appoint or dismiss.

As we have said elsewhere, a school's bill for wages and salaries can amount to about 80 per cent of a school's expenditure. If finance becomes difficult, it is tempting to look to reduce the amount spent on that item. This is not as easy as it sounds because staff are very likely to be entitled to redundancy compensation like everyone else, and payment of this might make your budget problem even worse. Moreover it is frequently difficult to decide who should be selected for redundancy. *Redundancy is a very sensitive area in which governors should at all times take legal advice from County Hall or wherever.*

All staff of course can be dismissed on disciplinary grounds. Poor teaching (difficult but not impossible to prove), failure to carry out reasonable instructions, inefficiency, and poor time-keeping are examples of possible grounds. Every governing body however *must* have a code of practice agreed by the full governing body (not a sub-committee) and all staff must be informed of its existence. It is likely to be appreciated if staff are involved during the development of the policy. *The most common reason for a dismissal action to go wrong is because governors had not drawn up a reasonable policy and stuck to it.* Failure to do this amounts to what the law calls 'unfair dismissal' and hefty compensation may be awarded. Usually formal warnings to staff, oral or written, are sufficient.

Policies on pay and staffing are both in the hands of governors. There has been interest in some political circles in settling teachers' pay and conditions locally, but since 1922 they have been settled nationally. In the case of county and special schools, governors must accept any conditions of service for their non-teaching staffs which have been agreed by County Hall. They cannot, for example, pay lunch time supervisory or caretaking staff more than in other local schools, unless they are working to quite different job descriptions. A particular point to watch is that staff who are transferred into working for private employers when, for example, your school cleaning is privatised, take with them their existing conditions of service. This has come out of European Union legislation.

Grant maintained, independent schools and CTCs may set their own terms and conditions. However, as the result of the European ruling mentioned above, if they 'inherit' staff from a previous school – for example, if a voluntary school becomes a city technology college – the new employer must respect the terms and conditions of the old.

What do teachers do all day?

Teachers in all schools, apart from independent and city technology colleges, work to the so-called 'Baker contract', named after the Secretary of State, Kenneth Baker, who introduced it in the late 1980s. Until that time teachers did what had to be done in school as the need arose. The idea that the job could be defined in some way was considered silly, even unprofessional. However, as schools began to change rapidly, as courses also began to change profoundly with the introduction of the National Curriculum and new examinations such as the GCSE were introduced, and as society started (as it does from time to time) to blame all its ills on schools, wrongly in the main, so teachers began to feel acutely over-worked and underpaid. The result was industrial action in schools – surprisingly, by teachers who had never before shown the slightest approval of any form of militancy. Part of the eventual settlement was the Baker contract.

Teachers must by law be available for work for 195 days in the school year. Five of these days are set aside for professional training. These are known as 'Baker days' or 'B-days', which has produced a joke or two. Within these 195 days teachers must be available for work for 1265 hours, the equivalent of a 37.5 hour week. They must *be available for work*, not necessarily work those hours: the vast majority however work for much longer. The 1265 hours are known as *'directed time'*. Teachers cannot be compelled to work for longer. Nor can they be forced to take any part in the school meals service at lunch time and are entitled to a reasonable break. Schools employ midday supervisory assistants (often known as 'dinner ladies') to look after things at lunch time. Many teachers help voluntarily to back up the authority of the dinner ladies where it is needed.

Lesson preparation, administration, marking of pupils' work, and anything done outside school to enable the job to be done efficiently inside school are *not* counted in the 1265 hours. The other jobs which make up a teacher's daily routine are also listed in the contract. A sad casualty of the contract and of low morale has been the sharp decline in out-of-school activities which used to be the jewel in the crown of UK schools, though the organisation *Education Extra* has worked hard to reintroduce schemes for activities for pupils outside of normal school hours. Teachers still volunteer, but the valuable work they do with children is not included in the contract.

Head teachers simply cannot afford to let teachers take a group of pupils for example to Switzerland for a week on 'directed time'. Since the teachers would be on duty looking after the children for 24 hours per day for 7 days,

168 hours would come off the 1265 hour maximum: the teachers might not have enough left to complete their teaching in school at the end of the year.

For these reasons head teachers now have to draw up a time budget. A typical one is given below. Governors need to be very aware of the implications for their school's time budget when asking for something to be done. The full description of teachers' duties is given as an appendix to this book.

SCHOOL TIME BUDGET (HOURS)

Timetabled week 8 periods × 35 minutes × 190 days:	887
Form periods, school assemblies 35 minutes × 190 days:	111
Duties before and after school 30 minutes × 38 weeks:	19
Breaks 25 minutes × 190 days:	79
Full staff meetings 6 × 1.5 hours per year:	9
Other staff meetings 2 hours × 38 weeks:	76
Parents' evenings 7 × 2 hours per year:	14
Appraisal	10
INSET days 5 days × 6 hours: **Contingencies**	30 30
Total:	**1265 hours**

Grievance procedures

Governors must by law have agreed procedures for dealing with grievances brought by the staff. The chief education officer needs to be consulted in the case of local authority schools: as mentioned above, it is the local authority which actually employs staff, despite the considerable powers given to governors.

Governors and the curriculum

The Education Reform Act of 1988 introduced a National Curriculum Governors and local authorities and the governors of grant maintained schools are required to see that it is implemented in their schools. Independent schools are not obliged to follow the National Curriculum. We shall cover the detail of the curriculum in Chapter 5, so in this section we concentrate on governors' actual responsibilities for the school curriculum.

City technology colleges have a clause in their funding agreement with the Department for Education which obliges them to 'have due regard' to the National Curriculum, and most follow it closely. Some CTCs have decided to work a longer school day than other schools, arguing that this gives them the opportunity to extend the curriculum for their pupils beyond the National Curriculum.

In addition to that, local education authorities are required by the Education Act of 1986 to have a curriculum policy as well. This must include the National Curriculum but can range further. Governors of local authority schools are bound by this, although the law permits slight local variations by governors. Voluntary schools must 'take account' of the policy. In all schools it is the head teacher who decides on the amount of time given to subjects, the timetable, organisation of classes, and the choice of teaching materials and equipment.

Political education

This is a curriculum issue which can inflame tempers. It is generally agreed that children should learn about the governmental and political system of the country they live in. It is part of our history. Since the 1970s, for example, the issue of UK membership of the European Union has been very much alive in the media and it is only reasonable that these issues will come up in school. Some schools nowadays weave a European dimension into the curriculum.

The law requires schools to teach about politics *in a balanced way*, giving opposing views, and governors are required to keep an eye on this in their school. The law, very unhelpfully, does not say how. Allegations of serious political bias should always be investigated. It needs to be remembered that good teachers may use discussion of the political system to get children to consider what freedom in a democracy means in practice. So long as they do this in a balanced way, drawing pupils' attention to different beliefs and ideologies does not mean the teacher is a political indoctrinator. In a democracy, devout Roman Catholics may see, for example, the defeat of the Spanish Armada in 1588 as a disaster for their faith, not a victory.

Primary school children must not be allowed to take part in *partisan* political activities, although they do need to learn what political parties are and what they stand for. Mock General Elections are acceptable.

Special educational needs

In drawing up their budgets governors need to consider the provision of different or extra facilities for pupils with special educational needs, often abbreviated to SEN. The term was first used formally in the Education Act of 1981. Children with 'learning difficulties' were to be 'statemented' as the Act put it: in other words they were to be assessed by qualified professionals, like educational psychologists, and a formal statement made of what their needs were.

Once this is done, there is a legal obligation on local authorities to see the needs are met. There is a belief that local authorities have not been keen to 'statement' children, fearing that they would not have the resources properly to care for them, or that 'statements' are often vague, so that nobody can point to anything specific and demand that it be provided. The intention of the Act was also that as far as possible children with special educational needs were to be educated in ordinary schools alongside ordinary pupils.

The Education Act of 1993 introduced considerable changes to the 1981 Act with a view to tidying things up. The Department for Education must produce a code of practice guiding local authorities in what they should do. Local authorities retain responsibility for statementing and providing for these children, whatever type of school they are in. Since 1993, however, the Secretary of State can fix the time in which statementing must take place and parents can, like all other parents, express a preference for the school they would like their child to attend.

If a school refuses to take a child, the Secretary of State can order it to admit the pupil. Although in a sense grant maintained schools are independent schools, local authorities have a right to visit pupils with special educational needs in them. Parents who object to a statement being made, or who object to what is in the statement, can appeal to a Special Educational Needs Tribunal. The Tribunal can send a pupil to a particular school.

Gifted and very able children are too often neglected in thinking about special needs. It is perhaps assumed that such children can cope without help, or, worse, that it would be wrong to allow them to excel. In general they often:

- have excellent memories
- prefer to work on their own and exhibit intense interest in the world
- enjoy solving problems and often produce original solutions
- learn very quickly indeed
- have a peculiar, though sometimes hilarious, sense of humour
- work to very high, self-imposed standards
- are capable of intense and lasting concentration
- have great powers of imagination

Not all gifted children exhibit these qualities, but such children may become troublesome in class because they are bored. They can become day-dreamers or even cheeky for the same reason. The major difficulty they face is that many teachers fail to recognise these children for what they are, whereas disabled or dyslexic pupils, for example, are often, though not always, easier to recognise. Schools need a member of staff who is responsible for identifying such pupils. Teachers with this responsibility have frequently found it difficult to divert scarce resources to very able children and during financial setbacks their jobs have even disappeared. Governors have a critical part to play here.

GOVERNORS' POLICIES

There are a number of areas where governors need to have written policies.

Sex, race and physical disability discrimination

The main provisions of this legislation are by now well known, although it is surprising how many governing bodies seem to think quite wrongly that the Acts do not apply to them and their schools. Governors usually have policies on discrimination, covering staff, pupils, governors, parents and other visitors to the school. What provision does your school have, for example, for visiting parents who are confined to a wheelchair? How does your school react to the admission of very nearsighted pupils?

Increasing attention is being brought to bear nowadays on what the law calls '*indirect* discrimination'. This refers to discrimination which is quite unintentional and totally unforeseen. If a school were to advertise, to give a silly example, for a 'Teacher of science – applicants aged 30 or lower, able to sing bass in the staff choir, are preferred', this would be said to exclude women and older teachers. It would be sex and age discrimination, and there would be a great fuss about the former, and only slightly less noise about the latter. Governors acting on notions that only women can teach hockey, or only men coach football, could be discriminatory and doing what amounts to acting illegally. One school advertised for a 'site manager', arguing that the term 'manager' included the possibility of there being a 'manageress'. The question was asked: Would the term 'manageress', had it been used, have been taken by readers to include 'manager'?

Discrimination can also be involved in the appointment and promotion of teachers. The teacher's contract, as we have seen, defines what the limits of the job are. Teachers with families would be aggrieved if promotion went to an unmarried single teacher, solely on the grounds that such a type of person had fewer distractions. Promotions and appointments must be given on the individual's *actual* merit and suitability, not on the basis of stereotyping.

Where pupils are concerned, governors would be well advised to ask questions if it were found that members of a particular ethnic group figured *disproportionately* in punishments, suspensions or even permanent exclusions. It may be accidental: on the other hand, there has been considerable concern that black Afro-Caribbean boys have been excluded in greater numbers than other pupils.

An area of particular interest to teachers and governors is that of pupil choice. Why do girls more than boys seem to choose to specialise in languages in their early teens? Why, similarly, do far more boys than girls choose to study chemistry and physics at A level? Why does this happen much more in some schools than in others? What can the school do to keep all subjects equally open to boys and girls?

Governors, who after all have responsibility for the whole curriculum of their pupils, need to know some of the answers at least. Many governing bodies try to make the discussion of equal opportunities a mainstream rather than a marginal issue in their schools – for pupils as well as staff.

Sex education

This is a curriculum minefield for schools, and teachers and staff have to tread *very* carefully. This is because there is no agreement amongst parents about whether schools

- should teach about sex at all;
- if they do, how much and what they should teach about sex;
- should teach about homosexuality;
- if they do cover these, from what age they should teach various topics.

This is an issue which erupts from time to time in the media, most recently when the world grew alarmed at the spread of AIDS. This obviously brought into focus the issue of contraceptives and 'safer sex'. Governors will see that they may be in a difficult situation. Boarding schools in particular face problems, given that the school is responsible for its pupils 24 hours a day.

One reaction of the government to these concerns in the early 1990s was to move the issue of AIDS into the National Curriculum. Otherwise it is up to governors of primary schools to decide whether sex education shall be given in their school, and, if so, to devise a policy on sex education, obviously in close consultation with the staff of the school. Governors of secondary schools must ensure that sex education is given in accordance with their policy. Furthermore there is a requirement on schools to stress that sex is part of a close, loving relationship and not just a set of biological facts, necessary as those are. The sex education policy should be *in writing* and be available to parents to see.

One slightly zany concession to what was judged to be the public mood was a change in the law, permitting parents to withdraw their children from sex education in publicly-funded schools. Thus, if a primary school child asks his or her teacher 'Mr Smith, do you know where I come from?' the teacher should in theory say: 'Yes I do, Peter, but your mummy and daddy don't want me to tell you.'

Teaching about contraception is also fraught with difficulties since it is doubtful whether teachers, even if they know that children are sexually active, can legally give contraceptive advice without the prior knowledge of parents. This makes teaching about the prevention of AIDS difficult. Advice from the Department for Education on this matter has been widely attacked as unreasonable by doctors, nurses and other workers in the field of health education. Teachers are well aware that the same parents who object to their children receiving advice about contraception may one day turn on the school if their children produce babies. Teachers are most able to influence children when they have gained their trust. Some children will confide things in their teachers which they will not confide in their parents, and teachers are loath to break that trust by 'grassing'.

Teaching about homosexuality is sometimes seen as even more problematical for schools and governors. It cannot be known exactly, but about 10 per cent of an average school's population might have homosexual tendencies, sometimes as part of a growing-up phase ('falling in love' with a teacher or pupil of the same sex, for example), sometimes more permanently. Homosexual children have equal rights before the law to a suitable sex education, again in the context of a loving relationship. And homosexuals have equal rights to be governors, teachers and head teachers.

We believe that governors *should* have a policy on sex education and that each governor should have seen the policy and the teaching materials which are to be used, in case complaints are made to individual governors. Many schools use broadcast sex education programmes put out by the BBC and the independent companies, so that they can argue, if there are complaints, that thousands of other schools are watching the same television programmes. There is still no guarantee that nobody will complain, so it is best if governors and parents have themselves seen the videotapes.

School discipline policy

The head teacher is responsible for the day-to-day maintenance of good order and discipline in the school. It is helpful however to have a written policy which guides all staff and ensures a common approach – something which is more difficult to achieve in bigger schools. Otherwise one teacher may adopt one line, and a different one another. A good school policy would be drawn up by staff and governors and offer guidance on:

- whole school behavioural norms
- guidelines for pupil conduct – copies throughout the school
- good classroom practice by staff

"ITEM SIX ... SCHOOL DISCIPLINE..."

- departmental rules, or rules for particular activities, e.g. for laboratories, school trips
- reinforcement and support available to staff
- sanctions available to staff
- reactions to bullying
- the disciplinary chain, who does what
- emergency situations
- roles of senior members of staff in the disciplinary process
- recording of indiscipline, both internally to the school and externally to parents
- under what circumstances parents are brought in
- making amends
- procedures for exclusion from school.

Such a policy goes far beyond the traditional view of 'school rules'.

Salaries policy

As we have said above, teachers' salaries are laid down nationally. Independent schools, city technology colleges and grant maintained schools are not obliged to follow those scales, but most do – sometimes adding to them. At one time teachers progressed up their salary scale by automatic annual increments. If they were promoted to a post carrying more responsibility, they progressed in the same way up a different but higher scale. It was also possible for teachers to have allowances in addition to their scale salary.

In the early 1990s the government tried to make movement up the scale depend on merit as much as on age. Governors can stop an annual increment being paid, if they see fit, or can restore it, or move deserving teachers more quickly up their scale. The government also brought in specific 'merit pay' by which teachers earn more by being rated highly.

These changes make it necessary for governors to have a clear policy, which is known to all. Nothing undermines confidence or morale more than a 'hole in the corner' pay system where nobody knows the rules and head teachers, or you as governors, are suspected of having favourite sons or daughters. The most fraught aspect of this is the award of additional allowances and merit pay. The rules need to be explicit – that is, if you think you *can* identify excellent teachers for this purpose. It's another minefield.

Here are what we think are some ingredients of a successful wages and salaries policy.

- All staff categories at the school should be consulted about it.
- It should include a clear statement of what the policy is intended to achieve. This will cover for example the need to improve still further the education offered by your school, to ensure that all staff are properly valued and to further the school's development plan.
- It should seek to motivate and retain existing staff, as well as to attract recruits of high quality. It is possible to pay 'incentive allowances' for responsibilities beyond those common to the majority of teachers, or outstanding ability as a classroom teacher. They can be paid also for posts which are difficult to fill or where there is a shortage of subject specialists. But beware. What is likely to happen if that mathematics specialist you 'bought in' very expensively turns out not to be very good in the classroom?
- It should reflect the level of responsibility which staff undertake, and provide opportunities for career development.
- It should meet the needs of the management of the school.
- It should be based on clear job descriptions at all levels.
- It should ensure that all wages and salaries are reviewed at regular intervals.
- All increases in salary (including annual increments) should be subject to agreed procedures on quality control.

- There should be a mechanism for dealing with grievances about wages and salaries.
- The policy should be monitored by a governors' sub-committee reporting to the full governing body.

Teacher appraisal

The law requires all teachers in county, voluntary and grant maintained schools to be appraised, usually on a two-year cycle. As the overall employer of teachers, the LEA will draw up the principles of a scheme for its teachers; it is for the governors of grant maintained schools to draw up and implement their own scheme in accordance with the national regulations. In all cases appraisees (that is, the teachers being appraised) are entitled to know the details of the appraisal scheme which affects them.

Appraisal is intended to help teachers to improve. Even the good can get better. It is concerned with removing the obstacles which individuals feel are hindering improvement in their work. It should make everyone aware that their contribution is valued, and that the best use is being made of their talents. No one is going to talk freely about the weaker aspects of their work if they feel that their salary or even their job is 'on the line'.

Unfortunately the whole idea got off to a bad start with teachers in the 1980s, when the then Secretary of State, Sir Keith Joseph, made an unfortunate remark about 'weeding out the incompetents' – it became clear that government and teachers had different views. Since then teachers' views about appraisal have, to some extent, prevailed. Teachers are appraised by their head teacher or by a senior teacher nominated by the head, though in many schools a great deal of negotiation takes place about who appraises whom. The area covered in the appraisal is that of the teacher's job description. Appraisal reports then are drawn up and include action plans for each teacher.

These records are confidential. The appraisee has a copy, so does the head teacher. In the case of local authority schools the chief education officer may ask to see a copy. The chair of governors of a school may see the plans of action of the staff: this could be helpful, for example, in setting budgets for the in-service training of staff. Other governors may not see them.

The relationship of appraisal to teachers' salaries and performance is tricky. The Education (School Teacher Appraisal) Regulations 1991 say that 'appraisal procedures shall not form part of any disciplinary or dismissal procedures'. However the Regulations also say that 'relevant information from appraisal records' can be used to advise those 'responsible for making decisions on the promotion, dismissal or discipline of school teachers or on the use of any discretion in relation to pay'. This may, therefore, link to governors' policy for salaries.

Governors are involved with appraisal in that they must take part in the establishment and management of the scheme. In practice that will mean asking for progress reports. Governors will also have a hand in training and development plans arising from appraisal.

Admissions policy

Where governors are responsible for admitting children to their school, they must have a policy which is available for all to see. They can delegate the working of the policy to a sub-committee, but that sub-committee cannot *change* the policy. The box shows some typical extracts from an admissions policy.

GASWORKS VIEW COMPREHENSIVE

Arrangements for the admission of pupils

a Applications must be made to the head teacher *in writing* on or before (date). It may not be possible to treat late applications with the same freedom as those received earlier, if there is pressure on places.
b Applications are welcome from any area. The school does not have any pre-determined catchment area or zone. The governors however reserve the right to consider the pupil's likely travelling arrangements in reaching a decision.
c Pupils will be admitted at 11 without reference to ability or aptitude, race or gender. In assessing the suitability of the school for any prospective pupil, the governors will have regard to the need to provide effective education for all the pupils at the school and the efficient use of resources, as the law requires.
d The number of admissions at 11 will be … There will also be … admissions at 16.
e In dealing with any excess of applications over available places the governors will take into account

   • any family association with the school
   • any siblings already in the school
   • any medical or personal factors deserving special consideration
   • the need to preserve the all-ability nature of the school

Appeals

A parent whose application is refused will be notified of how to appeal.

Policy on school journeys

Pupils undertake all sorts of visits as part of the National Curriculum and during school holidays. Teachers frequently give up their holidays to accompany their pupils. They are less common than a few years ago, but still form an essential part of children's education.

The highlighting in the media of tragic injuries and deaths during school journeys, both at home and abroad, in recent years has emphasised the need for schools to take careful precautions before school parties set out. The history of parents taking legal action in such cases is a long one and thought given beforehand to staffing and planning, as well as to foreseeable hazards, is a critical factor in determining the outcome of legal action. In short, if the school has done all that was foreseeably necessary (though nobody can foresee absolutely *everything* which might happen), the school is safe.

In CTCs, grant maintained and independent schools it is the governing body which carries ultimate responsibility. It cannot pass the buck to its head teacher, because the function of a governing body is to *supervise its head teacher*, and failure to do so adequately does not create a good impression in court. It might in some circumstances even increase the compensation awarded. It may be necessary too from time to time to remind enthusiastic teaching staff that failure to get proper approval for a school journey might leave them alone to face the music if things go wrong. The reason for this is that you as governors might have to say: 'Sorry, but if you had asked us in advance, we would certainly have refused permission for this particular journey to take place.'

In county and voluntary schools with local management the governors may be required to authorise *all* school journeys on behalf of the local authority. The authority may define what sort of journey is to be approved by governors: it may be journeys of more than 50 miles, or those lasting more than a given period of time away from school. In particular governors must satisfy themselves that local authority policy is being followed.

An important point to note is that journeys which obviously involve a higher degree of physical risk – one thinks of canoeing, abseiling and rock-climbing, though probably not skiing – may have to be approved in advance by specialist staff at County Hall.

From disasters which have occurred, and for which schools have been held to carry some responsibility, it is possible to see the sorts of things to which governors should give attention before approving school journeys. Readers may not be aware that the much publicised cases have usually *not* been caused by faulty supervision: it is the many *unpublicised* ones for which schools have been held liable.

Staffing

Although many are happy to do so, teachers cannot be *required* to take part in school journeys unless the head teacher authorises it as 'directed time' (see 'Time Budgets' above). Local authority guidelines and legal precedent usually suggest no more than 10 pupils per teacher for school journeys abroad, perhaps 12 to 15 for journeys in the UK if circumstances suggest that this would be reasonable. If Wayne, Shane, Sharon and Esmerelda are all going (lovable, youthful, but well known for mischief) it is advisable to improve the staff–pupil ratio: it is *foreseeable* after all that their behaviour might not be good during the journey. Being able reasonably to foresee what might happen is part of a teacher's professional skill and knowledge of children. Some wag once remarked that planning school journeys was a kind of Forsyte Saga. And then there was the old hand who always stopped the coach a few miles short of the youth hostel, so that by the time the children had walked there, all they wanted was a meal and a good night's sleep.

Where large groups are concerned it is essential to divide that responsibility so the every child knows who his or her individual teacher-in-charge is. A group of 100 is actually more than twice as difficult to manage as a group of fifty, so *more* supervision is needed. It is unwise to travel away from school with only one teacher, in case the sole teacher is somehow separated from the group, has an accident, or, more likely, has to take a child to hospital. Visits to foreign countries with only one teacher should be firmly discouraged. Co-educational parties should have teachers of both sexes. If it is possible to visit the destination beforehand, it is advisable for the leader to do so, particularly where younger pupils are concerned.

Non-teachers

These, usually spouses, partners or parents, often accompany parties to make up numbers of adults. Be very careful here as governors, because *one adult does not automatically equal one teacher*. Parents and others are merely extra adults, not substitutes for teachers. For example, what would happen if the teacher in charge were suddenly to be taken to hospital, or separated from the party? If the spouse or parent is left in sole charge, are they fully briefed about the great responsibility they are carrying? Would they even go if they knew? Very importantly, how would the other pupils' parents react if they knew that Mrs Smith was to be in full charge? What if an emergency occurs? Ask yourself as a governor: 'Would *I* let my children go under those circumstances?'

Parents

Parents should be fully informed in advance about the journey. What if parents, teachers and pupils have to communicate with each other in an emergency when a party is in, say, Russia? A full address list and 'telephone chain' (who phones or contacts whom) is handy. It can help avoid the 'I would never have let Wendy go if I'd known that ...' Make sure parents sign an indemnity form. However, don't rely on it. If the supervision of children is demonstrably negligent, the form won't save you. Teachers and others in charge of children must behave responsibly and reasonably at all times. Make it clear to parents that this is not a do-as-you-please holiday. The party leader is in charge, and school and other rules will be enforced. Some schools require a parental signature to this effect.

Using outdoor centres

Make sure that these are on some *proper* approved list. The pupils will almost certainly be under the control of centre staff. You may not be able to meet the staff, but are you happy with their experience, qualifications and safety record? Beware of cowboys who pass themselves off as 'qualified' when they are not.

Financial matters

Money collected from pupils must be properly accounted for. Again, check that the firm you are using is on an approved list. Find out who is liable to parents if the firm goes broke or the holiday falls through for some other reason. It may be your governing body. Are deposits refundable by the firm, or can parents retrieve them from *you*? It is important to remember that parents are used to dealing with travel agents and expect a certain level of service.

In this connection there is a problem area of which governors need to be aware. The European Community Directive on Package Travel was originally introduced to protect consumers on package holidays against travel companies which go broke and close down. The Directive defines a travel organisation as one which sells together any two of tourist services, travel and accommodation, and lays down strict regulations. The snag is that a school which runs several journeys each year may well be a 'travel organisation' under these regulations. The position is not entirely clear, but it would be unwise of governors to act as if the Directive did *not* apply to them. The main principles of it are:

- Parents must be supplied with full details of travel, accommodation and insurance provided. It is criminal to fail to provide this or to give misleading information.
- The repayment of deposits if necessary must be guaranteed in all cases.
- Schools as travel organisers must accept responsibility and liability if things go wrong with travel or accommodation arrangements, or, worse, for death

or injury. Governors of all types of school need to look very hard at their insurance arrangements and take specialist advice.

The readiness of parents to take legal action has increased considerably in recent years. Accidents and mishaps which at one time would have seen as 'just one of those things' are now seen as actionable. It is perhaps not surprising that school journeys are nowadays less common than they were, but they are still very worthwhile if well organised.

Health and safety policy

Governors of local authority and voluntary schools will be covered by the local authority's policy since as the employer it has what the law calls a 'duty of care' towards its employees. However some of the policy will be delegated to governors and it is important that governors know what that is. Governors are responsible among other things for the purchase and maintenance of fire-fighting equipment to the agreed standard. They are also responsible for seeing that access to the premises is safe for everyone likely to be using them, i.e. parents and visitors, as well as children.

The governors of grant maintained and independent schools, like the governors of city technology colleges, are responsible for creating and implementing a health and safety policy, and for bringing it to the attention of their employees. The policy should cover all potentially injurious situations in schools and adopt best practice. It should cover the detail, for example, of the storage of chemicals in science laboratories, fume cupboards (which can be expensive items) and regular fire drills, which should be recorded.

Charges and remissions policy

Reference was made earlier to the charges which schools make to parents. Governors must by law have a policy about the charges their school makes. The policy must cover also the remission of charges in suitable cases, specifically in the case of families receiving income support or family credit. Remission is often necessary in cases where some pupils simply cannot afford to join their friends and classmates on an educational visit.

After reading this formidable list you may have resigned! However, do read on, as we now come to the exciting bits, describing how you can carry out your duties effectively.

Chapter 3

Being an effective school governor

If a governing body is to be effective then a group of individuals, some of whom may never have met before, must become a team and set out to work for the good of the school and its community. This implies keeping up to date about what is going on in education generally and in the school in particular, and pooling the talents and knowledge of politicians, parents, teachers and others in the locality to facilitate the successful running of the school. In this chapter we consider the roles of various kinds of governor, how governors can be trained, and what they can do to help schools.

POLITICAL NOMINEES

The governor chosen by a political party to serve as a local education authority nominee can be in a difficult position. Most people directly involved in schools – parents, teachers, pupils – do not see education in political terms at all. Although this can be said to be a naive view of life, it describes the vantage point of a sizeable chunk of humanity. Whether political party X or election manifesto Y is for or against some educational proposal is largely irrelevant unless it affects their own school. The tendency in some areas to nominate political governors entirely from one party is greatly resented by many people.

Consequently political nominees may be viewed with some suspicion by other governors for several reasons. They may be seen as 'professional' governors, serving on more than one school's governing body whilst not especially committed to any one of them, whereas parent or teacher governors see themselves as concerned only with the one school. They may be regarded as outsiders, perhaps not even living in the area and therefore not knowledgeable about local problems. Worst of all they may be perceived as 'lobby fodder', blindly following the national or local party political line on issues irrespective of the arguments surrounding them.

Political nominees face a dilemma on some occasions. They may discover that the governors' view of an issue is the opposite of that held by their political party. They must then use their judgement about how best to act.

The strength, on the other hand, of the politically nominated governors can be that they have often accrued great experience of local government, understand the workings of County Hall, and may be a member of some of its key committees, have served on other governing bodies, may have considerable local, regional and national knowledge on certain issues, and have been democratically elected to serve the people, albeit sometimes after a low poll. There is no universally agreed blueprint for success, but the following pieces of advice may be helpful to politically nominated governors.

Do

- Use your knowledge of local government to help fellow governors. If you are also a member of other local government committees, help your school there as well.
- Try to treat each school as special, even if you belong to more than one governing body. Empathise with parents and teachers, totally committed to 'their' school.
- Remember that the relationship between schools and the LEA has changed, and that LEAs no longer have the power over schools which they had in former times.
- Attend regularly, not just when something controversial is under discussion.
- Admit you are not too familiar with some issues under consideration, even if you have been on the education committee for years. Councillors who feign great wisdom about everything are rapidly rumbled; those who are willing to learn, no matter how experienced, are greatly respected.

Don't

- Blind your fellow governors with procedural wizardry. Most are amateurs at committee work and do not like to feel humiliated if they speak out of turn or do not understand committee ways.
- Toe the party line blindly. Think about each move. If you were elected on a 'save money' ticket, remember that education does cost money, and help to avoid waste rather than squash every initiative. Don't jump to conclusions about what 'waste' is. Find out!
- Fight the governors higher up. It is two-faced to be silent at a governors' meeting and then oppose their proposal at the education committee or elsewhere. Speak your mind at the governors' meeting, then if you argue against the issue subsequently people will respect your openness.
- Over-play the caucus by always voting as a block because you and your colleagues have decided to stick together on every issue on an 'LEA versus the rest' principle.
- Constantly compare the school unfavourably with others you know. It is

unfair when few people present can verify or refute your statements. There is a diplomatic way of letting fellow governors know what other schools of your acquaintance do in similar circumstances to the ones under discussion.

PARENTS

Parent governors have been elected by the body of parents, many of whom may not know their nominee even by sight. It is quite a good idea for parent governors to give some thought to this problem. For example, there is no reason why parent-governors should not be introduced at meetings of the parent–teacher association, if there is one, or at a parents' evening. It simply requires the person running the meeting to ask the parent governors to stand up and be seen. We are all used to seeing a couple of self-conscious beetroot faces surface briefly and then subside amid good-natured and curious banter. 'So that's him, then. Don't like his tie', is just one of the hazards of being, however modestly, in public life. Similarly a recent photograph and the name of each parent governor can be put on a poster and displayed prominently when there is a meeting of parents. There is no point in having parent governors and then not knowing who they are.

Representing the parents' point of view, when any school's parents may represent all conceivable views under the sun on any issue, is not straight-forward. It is helpful, therefore, if parent governors try to get around their 'parish' making sure they listen sympathetically to opinions which conflict with their own. Parent governors who speak only for themselves or for the benefit of their own children become notorious. A parent arguing strongly for favourable treatment of one group may, by implication, be arguing for less favourable treatment of another. For example, if the parent of a keen gymnast pressed for classes of four in gymnastics, the parents of dance enthusiasts might find their children in a class of forty.

One way of communicating with parents is to ask the governors to agree to the school distributing a newsletter to all parents whenever they send out a mailing. Schools often send letters home about plays, concerts, open days or parents' evenings and one extra paper can easily be added. It can be translated into other languages if the school serves a multicultural community. A brief chatty letter might read something like this:

Dear Parent

You may be interested to know one or two things which have been happening at governors' meetings recently. At our March meeting the head teacher explained about the latest arrangements for national tests. There will be a meeting for all parents early next term to discuss this.

One of us was part of the appointment committee which chose Mrs Henderson as our new Head of Maths. She will be joining us from South Exchester High School starting in September.

Some parents have mentioned the dangerous crossing at the corner of Milton Street near the school entrance. We have raised this and been told that road alterations will soon make it much safer, but that in the meantime a lollipop lady has been employed.

We should like to remind parents about visits to the parents of new children in the summer. Last year 25 parents volunteered to visit the parents of all children coming into the school to see if they could answer questions and it was very successful and much appreciated. This year we take in a lot of children from the West Exchester estate, and it would be helpful if about 30 parents could help. Mrs Tripp, chairman of the Parents' Association, will be asking for volunteers early in the summer term.

Finally we should like to give you early warning that two of us 'retire' at the end of this year, and so anyone wishing to be a parent governor should volunteer when the note about elections comes round. We have enjoyed the work and found it interesting, and we should be glad to tell anyone wishing to stand for election what is involved.

Yours sincerely,

Eileen Chandler
David Evans
Alice Stephenson

Remember the point made in Chapter 2 about confidentiality. Make sure that your fellow governors know when you are discussing issues with parents so that no confidences are breached. One further point to remember when soliciting parents' points of view is that it is too easy to report only the views of one's own circle of friends. It is often said that only middle-class parents volunteer for this kind of responsibility, which is partly, if not entirely, true. Thus anyone elected from the posh end of town ought not to report only the views of Rotary wives, or opinions gleaned from fondue parties or the golf club dinner dance. There is much to be said for parent governors being chosen from different parts of the school's catchment area, and it should be possible for the people elected to be sensitive to views from all sections of the community.

Do

- Become known to your constituents.
- Send an occasional newsletter.

- Represent all sections of the community, not just your own friends. Involve other parents in your work beforehand, don't merely tell them about it afterwards.

Don't

- Overplay the line, 'Well my son is in the school, so I got the inside story.' Nudge, nudge, wink, wink.
- Press your own children's case, either openly or sureptitiously, at the expense of others.
- Be afraid to speak if the meeting is full of apparent experts. You are there as the voice of parents, not as Britain's leading authority on curriculum development. Good professionals welcome a clearly expressed non-expert's point of view. In any case many parents are far more expert in their knowledge of children's learning and well-being than they realise themselves. On the other hand don't pretend you're an expert if you are not.

TEACHERS

Teacher governors can also find themselves in an awkward position. They should become members of the team like everyone else, but they are inescapably employees in the school, and may be seen by other governors to be biased in favour of their colleagues whenever anything about teaching comes under scrutiny. As they are also professionally knowledgeable in education they may be tempted to overawe fellow governors with their expertise, and nothing will kill discussion or arouse hostility more quickly.

Their own colleagues will expect to know that their views are represented, and to be consulted about key issues. It is not a bad idea, therefore, for a note to be displayed permanently on the staff notice board giving the names of teacher governors, so that all, especially newcomers, are clear who is acting in this way for them. The same section of notice board can display notes of information for colleagues about what is happening in governors' meetings, though confidentiality should not be breached.

Anyone volunteering to stand as a teacher governor should be clear from the outset about the pressures which may ensue. On a particular issue, for example, the majority of her colleagues may hold one view, which she is duty bound to report, and the head may hold a different view – so already the teacher governor's loyalties are divided. She may herself hold a third view, which she should be as free to express as any other governor present.

As suggested in the section on parent governors above, she should respect confidentiality and try to discover the views of all her colleagues on matters, not just those of her personal friends or like-minded individuals. One way of doing this is to raise appropriate matters at staff meetings, so that both she and the head can try to interpret staff views. Whilst it is not a bad idea for the head and the teacher governors to consult before governors' meetings, it is not advisable for there to be such powerful collusion that the rest of the group feels threatened by a professional conspiracy.

The teacher governor should not be made to feel by the head that blind unswerving loyalty is demanded irrespective of her own views, and that any mild dissent is a serious breach of professional etiquette. On the other hand the teacher governor should not seek to embarrass the head deliberately, nor to win victories in the governing body denied to her in staff meetings, unless there is a serious problem of disharmony and lack of confidence in the senior people within the school.

When matters to do with individual members of staff are raised, teacher governors often withdraw. (They are sometimes required by the Articles to do so.) It is as well to minimise the occasions when any governor has to withdraw, so that the group can act as a team; and indeed it is an important aspect of professional life that people have to learn to keep a confidence, act fairly and humanely, and not press their own special interest at the expense of their colleagues.

On the other hand when a teacher governor's own affairs or a matter of direct concern to her are being discussed, she should always, in her own interests, be asked to withdraw. Just as a teacher governor should not be granted special privileges because of her position on the governing body, so too she should not be any worse off.

The following summarises some of the points made above:

Do

- Keep all your colleagues reasonably in the picture, using notice boards and meetings as necessary.
- Represent all views when asked, not merely those of friends or people with whom you agree.
- Express your own point of view, even if it conflicts with the majority view of your colleagues; you have that right the same as anyone else present.
- Discuss first with the head any issue on which you suspect you may wish to disagree with her. You are entitled to hold contrary views but out of courtesy you should let her know if possible.

Don't

- Dazzle fellow governors with technical jargon. Better to carry your real or imagined expertise lightly. This means avoiding phrases like 'Research has proved that . . .' (it rarely has).
- Feel threatened if one of the parents has a child in your class. Carry on normally.

- Press your own, your best friend's or your department's case unfairly when other colleagues are not present to put a contrary point of view.
- Dismiss the views of the lay people on the governing body. They may be contrary to current orthodoxy, but they should be listened to.
- Feel you have to justify everything the school does. Good schools constantly review their practices. Although other governors might be alarmed if you never had any confidence in what the school was doing, they will understand that issues in education are not always black and white, and that honest self-doubts can sometimes produce healthy changes.
- Serve for ever. Allow colleagues to have the experience, even if they wish to re-elect you. It is good for the job to be shared amongst several teachers over the years.

THE HEAD

Heads have a vital role to play in any board of governors. Poor relationships between the head and the governing body can affect the running of the whole school and are, fortunately, relatively rare, being usually a symptom of some deeper problem when they occur. There is everything for the school, and indeed the community, to gain when relationships between head and governors are good. As we pointed out in Chapter 2, the head's report is often an important part of the meeting, other governors being very dependent on him to keep them up to date with what is happening. Governors appreciate honesty here, being unconvinced at hearing nothing but games results when everyone knows there are problems elsewhere.

Most governing bodies look to the head for a clear lead on almost every issue which occurs, and it is as well not to be too defensive and try to prevent governors asking searching questions. The 'clever' head who approaches meetings too slickly, because he believes governing bodies are a nonsense and only need proper handling to make them totally innocuous, does himself and his school a disservice. Successful heads involve their governors in the life of the school whilst not ducking their own responsibilities.

The balance between the paid professionals, hired to take front-line responsibility for running the school, and the governors, unpaid amateurs charged with certain responsibilities and expected to show interest in the school in general, is perhaps a difficult one to strike, but many heads have done it to the satisfaction of all concerned, and without the need for an elaborate rule book or demarcation procedure.

In summary:

Do

- Be open and above board about successes and problems; it will usually be appreciated.
- Establish good rapport with the chairman in particular.

- Express your own point of view, even if it conflicts with that of the rest of the staff.
- Encourage governors to be actively involved in the school in some way, not just attend meetings.

Don't

- Dazzle governors with technical expertise.
- Blackmail the teacher or parent governors by looking hurt if they disagree with your views.
- Feel threatened if governors offer positive suggestions. If they are bad explain why you cannot use them; if they are good seize them with alacrity. No individual has a monopoly of wisdom.
- Boast to your colleagues that you have your governors sewn up. They may grass on you.
- Deride councillors and lay governors. They are trying, in the main, to perform a public service, and are often delighted to be asked for help.

PUPILS

When pupils attend governors' meetings as observers, which they have to be, since they cannot be full governors, the chief complaint voiced about them is that they rarely join in discussions. Clearly there are difficulties when an inexperienced adolescent finds herself amongst adults, including her own teacher and head and several leaders in the community.

Nevertheless pupils can and do perform a useful function, and much of what is said above applies to them: that they should try to speak for their fellow pupils, not merely give their own point of view, that of their friends or their own age group, and that they should keep other pupils informed about governors' meetings, except when confidential matters are involved, though usually they will not have been present for such business.

Teachers should take seriously the role of pupil observer, and, without reducing the pupil's role, help her to do the job properly by explaining about procedure, giving relevant background information and letting her produce a newsletter for the notice board. Handled well the experience can be a piece of sound social education, both for the pupils directly involved and for the whole student body.

CHAIR

The chair and vice-chair of governors sit in a very important and influential position. They are responsible for setting the tone at meetings, and can be an important lubricant, establishing communication between themselves and the head, and between the governors and the LEA. The role of chair is dealt with more fully in Chapter 4.

CO-OPTED GOVERNORS

Some governors are recruited because of a special role they play in the community. They may, for example, be experienced in the world of industry, the church, farming or the social services. They can bring a dimension to the governing body which other members cannot readily give. It is important that they use their strengths for the benefit of the school. It is useless if someone co-opted from local industry never shows interest, or merely turns up to meetings to air time-honoured prejudices about education. On the other hand someone who forges links with the world of work, and advises about the use of buildings, financial matters or careers, can be a treasure.

Employers of co-opted governors can help by allowing their employee some time off and by not docking their salary on the few occasions they may need to take a little time off work for school business.

ADMINISTRATORS

What has been said above about teachers and heads applies to professional administrators, such as Area Education Officers, who attend governors' meetings acting as clerk: they should not overplay the role of 'expert'; not evade issues by exploiting their knowledge of committee procedure or the complexity of County Hall; not dress up their own prejudices by falsely claiming them to be government or county policy. And they should report practice at other schools, not to disparage a particular school but to inform discussion.

TRAINING FOR GOVERNORS

There are several ways in which governors can be trained to do their job effectively. Many local authorities have been running workshops for governors for several years, some lasting a half or a whole day, others spread over a residential weekend, or comprising a series of sessions spread over a long period. Courses are sometimes put on for governors over a whole region, or mounted specifically for one or two governing bodies.

There is a great deal to be said for a carefully thought out policy on governor training. Amongst basic principles might be the following:

- *Involve the profession.* Heads or teachers might occasionally be hostile to training programmes if they fantasise that a squad of muscled heavies will descend on them bristling with expertise and tactical weaponry. If one involves heads in the training not only can they see what is happening, but they can give valuable advice.
- *Make it practical.* Let governors see curricular materials, tackle real cases which have come before governors, and role play imaginary meetings. Use

problem cases, like those in Chapter 7. Where possible use good video material such as that available from the BBC or the Open University.

- *Bring in as many as possible.* Training courses which only allow one person to attend from each governing body will take an age to spread and will never reach most people. If possible regional courses should be mounted for two or three representatives from each governing body, and local courses for a larger group of people from each school.

- *Provide back-up material.* Often people go to training courses and then find they cannot recall the details. A small resource booklet or pamphlet summarising the conference, a set of guidelines, letters of information or news sheets will give people a useful record of proceedings to which they can refer at leisure.

- *Follow through.* Often courses are put on and then forgotten about. Governors who have been to an induction course in the early stages of their governorship may have an appetite for something more exacting after a year or two. Furthermore it should be remembered that hundreds of new governors are engaged every year, in many cases for the first time in their lives. Thus a course run one year might have to be repeated every year or two to cater for all the newcomers.

A sample programme for a one-day induction course might look something like that shown in the following box.

9.30 a.m. *Introduction: Governors' responsibilities and relationships with the LEA*
Mr J. Thomas, Deputy Chief Education Officer
10.15   *Financial matters*
Mrs B. Davies, Accountant
11.00   Coffee
11.15   Working groups (lists on notice board)
Watch and discuss video on new curriculum initiatives
12.30 p.m. Chairs of groups to report back
1.00   Lunch
2.00   Split into two groups for primary and secondary governors
1 *Recent developments in primary education*
Mrs A Bowles, Head of South Exchester First School
2 *Recent developments in secondary education*
Mrs C. Jackson, Warden of Exchester Teachers' Centre
3.00   Tea
3.15   Discussion groups, deal with case studies A, B and C
4.15   Plenary session
4.45   Conference ends

Heads, university and college lecturers, advisers and experienced governors might act as group chairs, and the case material provided can be fictitious items based on real events, involving pupil suspensions, teacher misdemeanour, parents appealing against governors' decisions, financial aspects and so on. Follow-up sessions might subsequently deal with various new curriculum documents affecting schools, and introduction to County Hall, important national or local reports and any new Education Act. In addition to courses by LEAs, governors can inform themselves about new developments relevant to their job by showing a lively interest in what is written about education. This point is further developed in Chapter 5 and suggested reading is given on page 175.

LAY GOVERNORS AND THE APPOINTMENT OF STAFF

Governors are also involved in making appointments to the school staff, along, of course, with the head teacher and possibly a specialist adviser from County Hall. This is a most important assignment and we shall therefore discuss it at greater length. There is no need for you as a lay governor to feel that you have nothing to offer the experts. By the time things get as far as the interview, applicants with unsuitable professional qualifications will usually have been sifted out, and the appointment will probably turn around which candidate is likely to fit into the school and make the best contribution to all aspects of school life. Here a well-informed governor can have as much to contribute as the professional experts. On occasion, you might even score a point or two. On one occasion a lay governor, in private life a housewife, asked a very highly qualified applicant for a post teaching Home Economics why the subject was taught in school at all; after all, wasn't it up to parents to teach their children to cook at home? The candidate appeared not to have faced that basic question before and floundered badly, yet none of the experts present saw fit to ask it.

'Hire in haste, repent at leisure' is an old saying in the appointments business. A teacher may be appointed after an interview of no more than half an hour. He may spend the next twenty years doing untold damage to your school and your hopes. Time spent on the careful selection of a teacher is not wasted.

In general, it is a good thing that governors should be closely involved with new appointments. It is, for example, one way in which you can become involved with what is taught in your school and how. Equally importantly it provides an excellent way of getting to know the teachers. There are unfortunately a number of horror stories around of governors who ask idiotic questions or ride roughshod over the views of others, and such behaviour when it occurs embarrasses all concerned. Governors are now a regular feature of appointing committees, whereas a few years ago many appointments would have been made by heads acting alone.

During the 1980s and 1990s there have been large changes in the number of children in schools. Some schools find they do not have enough cash to employ all the teachers in the school, so some teachers lose their job. In order to ease the problem of redundancy, LEAs will do their best to persuade governors to fill teaching vacancies with teachers displaced from other schools within the authority. This could perhaps give you a headache. When a head is told that he must reduce his staff because of falling numbers he will not be keen to lose his best teachers first. He might even be glad to be rid of someone who can be traded off to another school. On the other hand, when the LEA is forced to close down a whole school, you might be able to pick up teachers who will be a real asset to your own school.

When a vacancy occurs

If you are asked to assist in the appointment of a new teacher, you should first discuss with the head what the vacancy actually is, and find out her ideas on the sort of qualifications and person she would like. Your options might be limited: if the need is to replace the one and only teacher of knitting, because pupils are half-way through an examination course, then there is no room to manoeuvre. However, if the vacancy is within a large department it might be possible to work in something new – say, computer studies in the mathematics department, or Russian in modern languages. You might even find it possible to start a new out-of-school activity with the assistance of the person you appoint. Teachers in primary schools are usually generalists, i.e. they teach a range of class subjects, but they may still be able to provide leadership and inspiration to their colleagues in a particular field, like science or humanities. In secondary schools they are usually subject specialists teaching history, science and so on. In our rapidly changing society it is often important that teachers should be flexible, and an ability to teach as part of an integrated studies team in humanities or environmental studies may be very useful.

You should also find out any other factors involved in making the new appointment. The school may need, perhaps, more women teachers to even up the burden of those school duties which can be done only by a member of a particular sex, though unless the work can only be carried out by a person of that sex, the Sex Discrimination Act does not allow employers to appoint or reject people on the grounds of their sex alone. The post might be more suitable for an experienced teacher if it involves difficult children, otherwise a keen young teacher straight from college or university might be just what you want. Perhaps the department needs some vigorous new ideas injecting into it, and so on.

Candidates for appointment always appreciate being given the opportunity to have a good look at the school and their prospective colleagues before they take a post. The best method is usually to hold interviews later in the day, and make it possible for the interviewees to spend the earlier part of the day looking around and generally talking to people. This arrangement pays handsome dividends, since some applicants who might have accepted the post on interview find that your school is really not for them and save everybody much wasted time.

Finally, look through the application forms of those to be interviewed in advance. Remember that they are personal and highly confidential documents, and intended solely for the interviewers. If you are in doubt as to what parts of them mean, ask the head to explain.

Do's and Don'ts at the interview

Here are a few suggestions. Allow the candidate to talk, and don't talk too much yourself. Find out what else, apart from his main subjects, the candidate has to offer your school. Games? Chess? Producing a school play? Stay away from discussing the candidate's politics or religion. Of course, if you are appointing a Religious Education teacher in a voluntary school (or, indeed, any teacher in a denominational school) it is permissible to question a candidate about his religious opinions and practice. Remember the Race Relations and Equal Opportunities Acts make it illegal to consider the racial origin or, generally, sex of applicants. Ask the candidate what he makes of your school after looking around. If he has nothing to say, he may be either not very wide awake or, worse, a creep.

Find out what he has discovered about the school in general before he came to interview. This will give some indication of how interested he is in your particular post. Ask him to talk about his achievements in his present post. Ask him to say why he thinks his subject should be taught in school instead of, say, learning to drive or snake-charming. If the candidate has had several posts, ask why. Perhaps he has conscientiously set out to gain wide experience, which is a good thing, particularly if you are looking for a senior appointment. On the other hand, it may mean that he never stays long enough to be rumbled, and may well leave you quickly too.

Watch out for outdated qualifications. A 'distinction' on a college course, or a first-class degree mean little if the holder has done little since he gained them ten years ago or more. Teachers, like doctors, should keep up with new developments in their field through further training courses, which are readily available if teachers are willing to invest their time and show interest. Beware of the 'I'm far too conscientious to leave my pupils to go on courses' argument: if engineers took that view an awful lot of bridges would fall down.

Read the references supplied carefully. It is often worthwhile to check that the most obvious people have been asked to support the application. Although an applicant is perfectly free to ask whomsoever he likes to act as his referee, it is clearly odd, for example, if a teacher quotes only the pub landlord and his uncle in ICI. If you have doubts on this score, ask the applicant during the interview.

Ask what the candidate would do in your school if he had a free hand. Ask him how he would provide in his teaching for the cleverest and weakest children. Find out his attitude to punishment and incentives for children.

Finally, always allow sufficient time at the end for the candidate to ask you any questions he may have. Appointments are a two-way process, and the candidate is entitled to interview the school, although people who do this too aggressively often irritate the interviewers.

Sometimes there can be recrimination after an appointment. 'Why didn't I get the job?', candidates may ask after the interviews are over. There have been some disasters when inexperienced governors have attempted to give an answer. 'Your references weren't very good' is guaranteed to produce an angry reaction from both the candidate and the referees, who will complain about breach of confidentiality. Keep private notes on why the successful applicant was appointed. These can be invaluable if there are any queries or complaints afterwards, particularly in the areas of racial and gender discrimination.

Remember that if you are asked to take part in an appointment it is one of the most important tasks you will have to do as a governor. Remember, too, that the people coming for interview are usually highly trained professionals who may have to uproot their family if you appoint them, and who may have travelled a considerable distance to attend for interviews. Interviews should be searching but sensitive affairs.

HELPING THE SCHOOL

We asked a number of heads how governors had been particularly helpful to their school. We heard many stories of good support, and this was particularly marked when governors, despite their different backgrounds, acted as a supportive team rather than as a set of disparate individuals.

They told us of parent governors who mobilised other parents to visit the houses of new pupils; of business governors who persuaded their colleagues to provide work experience, raised money to help finance pupils' projects, or helped arrange mock interviews for older students about to enter the job market; of political governors who took on County Hall and their own political party; of governors who came along to school-based in-service courses to see what was new in education; of those who supported the school in the face of a malicious newspaper report.

The other side of the coin is equally illuminating. Governors spoke appreciatively of heads who kept them in the picture, of local authorities who put on interesting courses, of teachers who were open and honest about successes and problems and did not put obstacles in the way of governors trying to do their job.

Sadly there was also a negative element. Heads told of governors who only turned up to torpedo whatever was suggested; of the governor who opposed the head's release for an in-service course on the grounds that heads should already know all there is to know; the one who stormed into the school announcing she had just been made a governor and had come to inspect; the governor who insisted on helping in the classroom and bored the class to tears with long-winded stories; the one who, because he was a lawyer, claimed expertise on everything on the agenda; and a number of bad chairs who ruled autocratically, failed to take advice and were insensitive to nervous parent or lay members.

Unhappy stories from governors concerned, for example, the head who constantly reminded them that they knew little about education and that he was really in charge, or who said he would consider each suggestion and then quietly forgot about it; the teacher governor who saw every proposal as an attack on the profession; the administrator who never gave an opinion, but always said he would have to consult his colleagues or the great Chief Education Officer in the sky; and the local authority that kept telling governors how important they were, but never gave any direct help or advice.

In general, however, there were many happy stories, a few miserable ones and some total catastrophes. The greatest enemy appeared to be apathy. There are considerable demands on governors nowadays, and it is best to tackle them in a businesslike and cheerful way. Hand wringing is all very well, but merely complaining that times are hard, so there's not much anyone can do, will not solve the many problems facing schools.

There is an important and valuable function for school governors to fulfil and it is the collective duty of all the governing body, not just the head and chair, to see that the job is done sensitively, constructively and effectively. Whilst commonsense and goodwill alone will not ensure this, they will certainly lay a sound foundation. Anyone uneasy or uncertain about what the governors are doing can always ask the chair for a discussion of how the governors can best conduct their business to be a central item on the agenda.

Chapter 4

Governors' meetings

WHAT IS A COMMITTEE?

'Through you, Madam Chairman', 'Is there a seconder for the motion?', 'I'm sorry but I must rule that out of order'. People joining a committee for the first time are often surprised and even intimidated by the formality of language employed by members who, a few minutes earlier, were convulsing each other with funny stories, or calling one another Sid and Mary. There is thus a need for members of a governing body, particularly those who have not been in such a group before, to become familiar with committee procedure.

A committee is a group of people who meet occasionally or regularly to discuss matters in a certain field. It may be executive, i.e. able to make and possibly enforce decisions, or advisory. Most committees have been set up by some larger group of people and are therefore accountable to that group. Like governing bodies of schools they may be both executive and advisory, given delegated powers to make many decisions without reference back to the larger group, in this case the LEA, but sometimes acting in an advisory capacity. It is often when a committee exceeds its powers that problems are created.

This pattern can be extended still further. Most committees will at some time set up an even smaller group of themselves as a *sub-committee* to do a particular job for which the larger group might be too cumbersome. The sub-committee will then report back to the main committee. In governing bodies this typically happens over matters like staff appointments, as was described in Chapter 2.

Certain assumptions are made about committees. They are not always fulfilled but can be described as general unwritten hopes when committees assemble. First of all it is assumed that business will be conducted in an *orderly* manner. Anyone who has ever been to a chaotic or acrimonious meeting will know how important orderliness can be. A committee will usually, therefore, have certain agreed procedures to ensure the smooth transaction of its affairs. It will have an *agenda* listing items of business, sometimes with supporting papers giving members background information; a *chair* who will organise the meeting, call on speakers, give a ruling when necessary, sum up, decide when to pass on to the next item and so on; and a *secretary* to make the notes which will eventually constitute the record of that meeting.

Secondly, because decisions often have to be made, it will be assumed that after discussion a *consensus* of members' views will be sought. If there is some doubt it may be desirable to put the matter to a vote. The common assumption is that members will agree to abide by the majority decision and that, if there is deadlock, the chair will give a casting vote.

Thirdly, there should be a sense of *collective responsibility*; that is, an agreement that, once a decision is made, members will not hereafter publicly dissociate themselves from it, but rather support it as a group, even if they themselves were against it in discussion. This convention is frequently broken, especially when an individual member feels especially strongly about some matter, or is mandated by the group he represents to advocate a particular point of view. If, for example, many parents press a parent governor to raise an issue which is subsequently defeated when put to the vote, it would be most unfair if that governor had to pretend that he totally approved of the decision. On the other hand, in the interest of group cohesion he should not be publicly aggressive about his disagreement, otherwise the governors cannot function as a unit, only as a collection of individuals or pressure groups. The best solution is probably for the dissenting governor to have his dissent recorded in the public minutes of the meeting.

Other conventions are also broken at times, for either good or bad reasons. Someone wishing to undermine a group may seek to have business conducted in a *disorderly* manner by constant interruption, refusal to accept the chair's rulings, or by speaking at excessive length. This kind of roguish inability to accept reasonable chairmanship is rare, and when it does occur, sometimes suggests that the chair has been unreasonable.

COMMITTEE PROCEDURE

To avoid people quarrelling with each other across the room remarks are normally addressed 'through the chair'. This can sometimes reduce acrimony. The angry exchange:

Speaker A: I never said you twisted the account of the last meeting.
Speaker B: Yes you did, you liar.

might, in strict committee language, go something like this:

Speaker A: I wonder, Mr Chairman, if Mr Bloggs could clarify what he felt was wrong with the version of events just given.
Chairman: Mr Bloggs, could you tell us a bit more about your objection?
Speaker B: I felt that minute 234 was not entirely accurate and should have read . . .

Skilful 'Black Belt' committee members can use committee procedure to generate hostility, anger or to scapegoat, and no amount of formal chairmanship will make a miserable group happy or a divided group cohesive. The question of formality is discussed again below.

So that members may make decisions and recommendations in the best circumstances, certain features of committee work are essential. First of all the location is important. Frequently meetings take place in dismal or cramped conditions, and it is impossible to avoid an air of seediness. Governors should be able to sit in reasonable comfort, neither perched precariously on infant-sized stools nor submerged in the sumptuous, sleep-inducing armchairs of the Alderman Harry Ramsbottom Committee Room.

The room should be decently lit and ventilated, so that members do not have to share the same limited supply of oxygen, and they should agree not to dine too well beforehand. Those who do so may lapse into slumber, which is not good for the chair's morale, and they should be awakened unless elderly, frail or more effective asleep than awake, as their eventual loud snore might turn out to be the decisive vote on an important item.

Certain bits of paraphernalia go with meetings. Most important of these are 'the papers', a twentieth-century form of magic, which incorporate the business of the meeting.

Minutes and agenda

Two vital pieces of paper are needed at each meeting. First of all there are the *minutes of the last meeting*, the record kept by the secretary of business transacted, usually in numbered form:

Minute 234: head's report

> The head reported on the period April 1st to July 31st (copy filed with minutes). Members noted with pleasure the growing interest in charity work and asked the head to convey their congratulations to the pupils and teachers involved. There was some discussion of the amount of time required to administer the GCSE examination. Governors expressed their regret at the low take-up of a second foreign language in Year 10, but were glad to note that the staff were very concerned and were taking action to see that more information would be given to pupils and parents about the choices available.

Minutes of meetings are kept together as a permanent record of the life of the school, and some schools have accounts of such meetings going back for hundreds of years. Consequently it is important that the minutes should be accurate. Governors should not hesitate to point out inaccuracies, unless these are tiny and immaterial, but it is not fair for members of a committee to insist that each of their own contributions and every brilliant turn of phrase be logged in. The minuting secretary has a difficult task encapsulating the spirit of perhaps twenty minutes of discussion into five or six lines without being harangued for omitting 'the bit where I said how important it was for the locker-room cupboard to be installed by Christmas'.

If everyone wants his own name in lights the minutes become not a record of the meeting but a literal transcript of it. A word for word transcript of a two hour meeting could run to thirty pages, would invade no bestseller list, and would lead to more Norwegian forests biting the dust to provide the paper. The best one should expect from minutes is a brief and accurate account, giving the flavour of the meeting and recording any decisions taken.

The second vital paper is the *agenda for the meeting*, which represents the batting order of items to be discussed. Certain time-honoured features regularly appear. A typical agenda, missing out the middle, might look something like the following box.

Meeting of school governors to be held on Thursday April 27th at 7 p.m. in the quiet reading room of the school library.

AGENDA

1 *Apologies for absence*
2 *Minutes of last meeting (February 10th)*
3 *Matters arising*
   (a) *Minute 234* Outcome of staff meetings on Year 10 options (Head to report)
   (b) *Minute 236* Deputation to County Hall on March 13th (Mr Jones to report)
   (c) *Minute 241* Delays to Cloakroom extension in south wing (Chair to report)
4 *Head's report*
5 *New housing estate in West Exchester* Governors will know that planning permission has now been granted for Messrs Botchett and Scarper to build 75 three- and four-bedroomed houses in West Exchester. A paper from the Chief Education Officer explaining possible implications for the school is attached.
12 *Date and time of next meeting*
   Thursday July 13th at 7 p.m. is proposed
13 *Any other business*

Usually the chair will begin by asking if members agree that the minutes of the last meeting constitute a correct record of events. He signs the filed copy when this is agreed, having made any necessary alterations first. 'Matters arising' allows the chair or any other member to update colleagues on the latest state of whatever was discussed last time. Sometimes certain matters for report are already included in the agenda, and members are then invited to comment on other relevant items as they wish. Unless there is a particularly pressing 'matter arising' the group normally passes fairly quickly on to the main body of the agenda, otherwise the meeting can never get itself moving ahead.

Newcomers to committee work never understand how the agenda is assembled. Some secretaries or chairs of committees circulate members in advance asking if there is anything they wish to raise, others assemble the agenda themselves. It is wise to make known how members may introduce an item, the deadline date for typing and distribution and so on, otherwise a sense of frustration develops, or else thorny issues are introduced unexpectedly under 'any other business'.

If you, as a governor, wish to raise an issue it might be helpful to provide a short paper to support the case. People are sometimes unnecessarily inhibited when asked to provide a paper, assuming that a great literary masterpiece is essential, or alternatively that a lengthy document with footnotes and tables is required. A supporting paper is often quite brief, and serves to let other members know in advance what the item is about. For example if an item simply appears as:

6 School uniform

no one knows what is involved. Is there some move to abolish it? Do people wish to change the style of uniform? On the other hand if the item appears as:

6 School uniform
(paper from Mrs Jenkins attached)

and a short covering note in simple, plain language from Mrs Jenkins is available, like the one in the box opposite, governors both know what is to be discussed and can find information or think of ideas in advance.

For similar reasons, when items come from the head or the Chief Education Officer they frequently have a paper attached, and governors should be familiar with the background to each item before the event. The only situation worse than a meeting where some members have clearly not even glanced at the papers, is when the chair is in this position.

Sometimes the item 'any other business' does not feature in an agenda. This is because members may in the past have raised controversial matters under this heading late in a meeting, with no one in possession of the appropriate information. If a member wishes to raise something, whether under this heading or not, after the agenda has appeared, it is customary to ask the chair's permission in advance. He may then rule whether it is appropriate to take it

---

SCHOOL UNIFORM

At a recent PTA meeting the question of the high cost of school uniform was raised. Parents were not against school uniform, but were worried at the expense involved, particularly to parents with two or three children at the school. The head and staff were very sympathetic, and we agreed that it should be given some thought before next year. One possibility was that any red cardigan or jumper should be allowed, not just the expensive ribbed one. Another suggestion was that we might somehow help parents buy second-hand uniforms from each other. One person thought that a grant was available to help parents with a low income, but no one seemed sure. Knowing that one governor was a social worker and another a teacher at a school that had tackled the problem already, we thought it would be a good idea if I, as a parent governor, raised it at a governors' meeting. Both the head and chair have agreed to this so I hope we can spend a few minutes on it. The head and PTA committee have said they are quite happy to look at any suggestions which come from this meeting.

Edna Jenkins

---

at such late notice or whether it should be deferred until the next meeting. In fairness to all other governors, members should try their best to have all important items put on the agenda in the proper way and in good time. If someone tries to bring up an important matter under 'any other business' when several members have already left, propose that it be deferred until the next meeting.

REACHING DECISIONS

Some items on the agenda need a decision and others merely require an airing. When a firm decision is needed it is common for the chair to interpret the mood of the meeting. Where there has been clear agreement the chair will often ask 'Do we agree then that . . . ?' or 'Am I right in assuming that no one is in favour of . . . ?' Where the feeling of the meeting is not clear-cut a vote is usually taken.

Formal procedure over voting can sometimes become a little complex. Normally members will be told what they are voting on, and if anyone is not clear what the issue is he should ask for a statement from the chair. Normal committee procedure requires one member to propose a motion and another to 'second' it. Once the wording has been agreed the chair asks for a vote: 'All those in favour please show . . . all those against . . . abstentions . . . I declare the motion carried by 12 votes to 8, with 2 abstentions.'

Life becomes complex when members disagree over the wording of a motion and wish to propose amendments. Thus someone may say, 'I disagree with the motion as put, could we vote on an amended version and add the phrase "provided he has not made a request during the previous twelve months"?' If a seconder is found the chair will usually put the amendment to a vote first to see if it is acceptable or if members prefer the original motion. It is up to members of a committee to make sure that such constitutional matters do not become silly. Most governors want to discuss the issues, not train for *Mastermind*.

It is the chair's duty to make sure that any formal proposal is clearly worded, not saturated with negatives and ambiguities. Most people operating at sub-genius level would not be certain what a 'Yes' or 'No' vote means with a motion such as 'We deplore anyone refusing to do nothing.' It is far better to vote on a positive version of a motion so that those voting 'for' or 'against' are crystal clear about what they are supporting.

Once a vote has been taken the strength of the voting is often important. A group will have more confidence if the vote was clear-cut than if it was close. When the voting results in a tie the chair may give a second, or casting, vote. Some chairs always give a casting vote *against* any change on the grounds that a tie does not constitute a majority in favour of change and things should therefore stay as they are. This stance is only really justifiable, if at all, if the chair has no strong feelings on the issue. The chair is usually an important person and if she has any views at all she should not hesitate to air them. The risk that some unpopular issue might become widely known as having been approved 'only on the chair's casting vote' is one of the hazards a chair must occasionally face up to when agreeing to take on the assignment. She can be reassured that chairs universally have to take on such responsibility, and that it is relatively rare for the casting vote to be needed. No one should castigate a chair for exercising her duty to resolve a deadlock.

GROUP DYNAMICS

There is something about the chemistry of a group of people meeting together which defies perfect explanation, even though a great deal of work has been undertaken studying such groups. Studies of group dynamics are far too numerous to mention here, but some aspects are of interest.

Small group dynamics are different from large group dynamics. In larger groups people will often have less time to speak and there will be more silent members. Some participants will be under pressure to utter views they do not really support because they are aware that it is sometimes more important to have been seen to state a point of view than actually to believe in it. For example, a parent governor might have to voice 'the parental view' whilst privately disagreeing with it. Smaller groups are usually much more informal and decisions are negotiated more casually. Few family breakfasts involve someone proposing and seconding a motion of censure on whoever buttered the toast.

Studies of groups have shown that people frequently play a regular and predictable role in them. There is often a *social welfare* person who switches on lights, turns heating up or down, suggests it must be time for coffee or that a window needs opening. A *joker* can help relieve tension by making people smile, or occasionally heighten it when his funnies misfire. A *guardian of the nation's morals* may remind members that doom is around the corner, that levity will not do, and that sombre faces should be the order of the day. An aura of perpetual sin hangs round such a person, contaminating the rest of the group who feel guilty without being able to say why. A brisk and businesslike *efficiency expert* may always be hustling the chair on to the next item. There are many other stereotypes.

Similarly in some groups people regularly have an expectation of time, and often fill it with remarkable accuracy. If eight people meet regularly for an hour, one person may talk for twenty minutes, another for ten, yet another remain silent. If for some reason the twenty-minute person is silent for the first half hour he is then under considerable pressure to dominate the last half hour and obtain his ration of talk.

Position in the room or around the table is also a feature of many groups. Without realising it, people who disagree with each other frequently choose places opposite one another and avoid adjacent seats, on the grounds that it is very difficult to sustain an argument with someone sitting at your left ear. Similarly those who share views often sit together and a concerted set of arguments for or against an issue will appear stronger coming from a cohesive group of three or four people. On the other hand, super-shrewd operators sometimes deliberately seat themselves in different places around a table so that an impression of general group agreement on an issue is created.

Why some groups manage beautifully and others never get off the ground is very difficult to explain. Certain features which kill groups stone dead are well known. One very aggressive member can spoil meetings and sensitive individuals subjected to a personal attack from such a person may never reappear or rarely speak thereafter. Amongst killers of good group interaction are the following stereotypes. Although caricatures, they are alive and well and often do not readily respond to hints, though you could try circling the appropriate description in this section of the book and leaving it open at the culprit's seat with a note signed 'A friend'.

- *The bad listener* never hears what others say because he is only waiting for a gap in the discussion to enable him to make his own contribution. This frequently is a repetition of what someone has already said.
- *The 'expert'* can be a pain in the neck, particularly if he is not really an expert at all. The person who once built himself a back porch should not pronounce loftily on all building matters, particularly if it fell down. One

governing body had to suffer the pontifications of an elderly lawyer. As the sole university graduate in the group he constantly spoke inaccurately on examinations or further and higher education from the basis of hopelessly out of date memories of his own early days. Even real experts can inhibit discussion by appearing to rule on every topic, but fortunately many genuine experts carry their learning lightly and do not overpower their fellows. Perhaps some of the worst offenders, unwittingly, are governors who are teachers at another school, and seek to make the school a replica of their own. A good and sensitive 'expert' on the other hand, whose views are valued by others, can be absolutely invaluable.

- *The Mona Lisa* sits silently throughout meetings wearing an enigmatic look and simply puts pressure on others to do all the talking. It is refreshing to have members who do not waste words, but governors who never say a single word on any issue for meeting after meeting are often making little contribution unless they are active behind the scenes. Better is an occasional well thought out statement at the appropriate time.

- *The windbag* can be a serious problem because he prevents others from speaking by enjoying his own contributions so much that he never shuts up. All governors may make a lengthy contribution or series of statements at some time or other, but this is not windbaggery. What distinguishes the windbag is that his speeches are repetitive and tedious, often rambling off the point. Skilful chairs have a number of strategies to handle the situation, but even 'May I just interrupt you a second and ask you to sum up?' can spark off another fifteen minutes.

- *'Little me'* uses disarming statements like, 'Well, of course, I don't really know anything about these matters', and then, having spent all night in the reference library, goes on to reel off official statistics for the last twenty-five years.

- *The 'Hear! Hear!'* is usually half asleep, and says the phrase indiscriminately, often inconsistently, nearly always after someone has spoken loudly.

Finally it should be said that when group dynamics go wrong it is the duty of every member of the governing body to make the group work. Rather than sit back lamenting about what a poor meeting it was, not speak because the level of debate is too low, or grumble about the boring agenda or lack of action, every member can help make a group a success. It should not be left to the chair alone to reduce acrimony, curtail rambling discussions or handle difficult members. If every person present exercises self-discipline, cares about the group and the school it serves, and acts unselfishly and in good faith, there will be few insoluble problems. Indeed, it is a testimony to the basic commonsense of the human race that most governing bodies are friendly and informal. The only reason that there is some concern in this section about problems is that happy groups will run themselves and problem-ridden groups need help.

THE CHAIR

The role of the chair in any committee is crucial. She sets the tone of the meeting, decides priorities, steers the group through the business and liaises with the head and LEA. No one should agree to take on chairmanship of a governing body unless she is willing to work hard to make a success of the job. It is also for stayers and not sprinters.

Many of the problems described above are avoided by skilful chairmanship, yet there are as many different styles of chairing meetings as there are chairs. The first aspect of chairmanship which should be of concern is that it offers considerable power to use or misuse. Thus the effective chair should be seen to be fair. That is not to say that she may not hold personal views, perhaps strong on some issues, but rather that her personal prejudices should not prevent her from listening to all sides of an argument and giving everyone a chance to contribute.

An autocratic style of chairmanship irritates members considerably. One powerful chair, whose style made Attila the Hun look like a moderate, once took a vote on an issue. There were twenty people present. 'All those in favour?' he asked. Nineteen hands went up. 'Well I'm against it,' he rejoined, and passed on to the next item.

One important choice for the chair is whether meetings should be formal or informal. If there is likely to be strife it is usually better to be formal and insist on contributions 'through the chair'. More often in governing bodies, however, an informal style is preferred. People frequently know each other already or feel more welcome in an informal atmosphere, especially if they are lay people unused to committee work. But informality does not imply sloppiness. If decisions have to be made and recorded then a certain formality of procedure is necessary; one cannot rely entirely on folk memory.

A good chair can perform several useful services. These include the following:

Pacing

If an agenda has ten or fifteen items she can consult with the head and clerk, using her judgement to see which seem to be important and which seem more trivial. Thus she might start by saying, 'Looking at the agenda it seems as if items 1, 2, 3 and 4 can be dealt with fairly quickly and items 5 and 8 ought to take a little bit more time. If people agree I propose we spend most of our time on items 6 and 7.' At this point members can indicate if they accord with this view, and someone will be free to suggest some other item as a high priority. The advantage of this approach is that it signals to the group where their efforts should be placed, so that they can help the chair move quickly through trivial items, and then debate more thoroughly the key issues. This avoids the problem of spending so long on early matters that later items which are important never receive proper attention. An alternative to this approach is not to make any decisions on priorities but keep a constant eye on the clock reminding people that 'we only have forty minutes left and still five more items to cover'.

Summing up

Often discussion becomes diffuse and difficult to follow. A good chair can help members considerably by giving an economical and fair summary, preferably from notes she has been keeping. She might, therefore, once in a while, say something like, 'Now is this a fair summary of what people have been saying? Most speakers seemed to be in favour of a small deputation to County Hall, but Mrs French was against that because of our experience last time. On the other hand some people thought that if we held a public meeting first and then went to County Hall, this would be better than last time when we hadn't prepared our case properly.' Other members can correct this version or agree that it is a fair summary of discussion to date. A good summary at an appropriate moment can often get a meeting out of a quagmire and move the group nearer a decision.

Ruling

There are frequently moments of uncertainty in committee meetings when people look to the chair for guidance. This requires her to give a ruling on some matter, as when someone says, for example, 'I know we're supposed to be discussing the unfilled teaching post but can we go back to our previous discussion on equal opportunities, or would you rule that out of order?' At this point the chair must use her judgement. Amongst many alternatives might be:

'No, I think we've spent enough time on that issue.'

'Well, only for five minutes at the most as we have rather a lot of business still to do.'

'Yes, I think that would be well worthwhile.'

'Would members like to spend a little time on that or should we press on?'

'Perhaps the head can advise us on this one.'

'Is there some particular point you wish to bring out briefly about our earlier discussion?'

There are many other possibilities. Provided that the chair is sensitive to the mood of the meeting most committees will accept a fair verdict, and even go along with an unpopular one, realising that business could never be transacted unless someone ruled on tricky matters. Chairs who run into difficulties have either been too heavy-handed or unsympathetic in their decisions, or else have dithered endlessly when everyone is quite happy to abide by a decision from the chair.

Manoeuvring

Most committees are clean and above board, some are riddled by chicanery. Sometimes it is hard to draw the line distinguishing socially acceptable manoeuvring from dirty tricks. Amongst many time-honoured tricks of the trade, recognisable and easily rumbled if decently handled, annoying and divisive if malevolently done, are the following.

Lobbying

When a person wishes to press a particular point of view he may rally support for it before the meeting. Usually this is a fairly honest procedure: someone approaches a fellow member saying, 'At the next meeting I'm hoping to persuade members to take some action over what I think is a very pressing problem. If I can just explain the background to you I hope you'll support me.' Occasionally the lobbying is more subtle or even obscure and certain dense, or for that matter shrewd, members of committees can sometimes accrue a fair number of free meals and drinks by not catching on quickly. Indeed, if lobbying were made an indictable offence tomorrow a sizeable group of exclusive clubs, pubs and expensive restaurants might go out of business. Too much lobbying reduces the spontaneity of meetings and can also embarrass members who feel obliged to support people when approached in this way, so as not to let them down.

Caucus

When a group of like-minded people wish to press a particular point of view or secure a certain decision, they sometimes meet as a group before the main committee meeting, and work out a plan of action. This is a fairly common occurrence, but it can be divisive, and it is often better to risk the spontaneity of unrehearsed meetings. For example if the parent governors, the political nominees, the co-opted governors or the head and teacher governors concert their strategies in advance it will be very difficult for the governing body ever to become a cohesive group. As we warned in Chapter 2, there is some sourness when the caucus group is in the majority, and non-caucus members find they have little to offer as decisions have been negotiated in advance.

Delaying

Sometimes people in a committee will delay the meeting deliberately to avoid discussion of a controversial item or to ensure fatigue and/or dwindled numbers when an important point is reached. Occasionally a chair will allow the group to dawdle over earlier items to cut short discussion of key later ones. It is up to other members of the group to be alert to this and ask if progress can be a little faster to ensure proper discussion of later items. Another common device is to set up a sub-committee and hope the problem will quietly be buried. Sub-committees should be used to do a proper job, not to dispose of something in an underhand way.

Horse-trading

When individuals or groups known to favour certain points of view are in conflict they will sometimes agree to do a deal in advance. One group will soft-pedal on one issue, the other on a subsequent one, thus allowing both groups some success. This is often totally bewildering and annoying to members of neither group who are utterly baffled by the lack of bite over what have previously been controversial matters.

Dirty versions of the above devices are really not necessary in any properly run committee, and indeed they bring great discredit to the notion of democratic involvement in decision-making. Judicious use of some of the tactics may be acceptable, but any governing body whose members obtain more satisfaction and pleasure from political manoeuvring than from properly looking after the welfare of a school and its community should stop and question why it exists.

MAKING EFFECTIVE USE OF COMMITTEES

Committees are often so stuck with the standard rituals they fail to exploit alternatives to battling through the agenda for session upon session. There are several quite simple and effective ways of conducting business which involve but minor amendments of normal procedures. A skilful chair can ensure that variety in practice makes meetings both interesting and enjoyable.

Buzz groups

Some members of a larger group experience frustration at not having an opportunity to speak. One way of releasing this tension is for the chair to allow the group to dissolve into buzz groups. At its simplest the meeting will be suspended for ten minutes or so whilst people gossip with their immediate neighbours without leaving their seats. Alternatively the chair may say, 'This is an important matter and everyone should have a chance to speak. Let's split into three groups of about six people and come back in half an hour. Perhaps one person in each group will report back when we re-assemble.'

Working-parties

When a committee has a particular job to do it may set up a working-party to guide it in its thinking. Whereas sub-committees tend to be more permanent, working-parties offer flexibility. Three or four people can be asked to meet fairly often to devise a solution to a problem or to fashion a proposal. Eventually they can present a report to the main committee at which point, their job completed, they may cease to exist. The ultimate fate of a successful working-party is to be made a sub-committee and live on indefinitely, like the characters in Sartre's *Huis Clos* who thought they were waiting to go to hell and eventually realised they were in it already, condemned to spend eternity in each other's company. At their best, working parties can do an excellent job in a way that a full committee never could.

Day conference

Committee members often feel fatigued particularly if they meet at the end of the day. Once in a while it is worth trying to find a whole day if this can be arranged. This can have a freshness about it, and also allow more time for members to reflect on issues. It is also good for group morale. A typical day's programme, using local resources, might look like the following box.

> *THEME*: CHANGES DURING THE COMING YEAR
>
> 10.00 a.m. Assemble for coffee
> 10.15   *Some changes the school faces*
>   The Head
> 11.15   Discussion in groups
> 12.30 p.m. Lunch
> 1.30   *Integrating children with special educational needs*
>   Mr Jackson, Special Needs Adviser
> 2.15   Discussion in groups
> 3.00   *The new technology guidelines, resource implications*
>   Mrs Thomas, Science and Technology Co-ordinator
> 4.00   Tea

Brainstorming

One way out of difficulty when a group has a problem and appears unable to reach a solution is to have a brainstorming session. The rules are very simple. Each member must produce as many ideas as possible, no criticism is allowed, and the secretary writes them all down. Finally all the ideas are considered more critically and any useful ones are adopted. The reason why a brainstorming session can sometimes, though not always, resolve a problem is simply explained. Some quite useful ideas often never reach fruition because they are criticised and discarded too early. Furthermore sometimes a great leap sideways is needed and solutions which initially seem silly can often be just what is needed. Think, for example, of all those early attempts to make aeroplanes. They failed because designers were stuck with the notion of birds and flapping wings. The idea of rigid wings or no wings at all would have seemed nonsense to people at the time, but this was precisely the solution needed.

Action notes

Often in meetings decisions are reached but no action ensues. It is easy for the secretary to the committee to devise a simple action note and send it to anyone who was asked in the meeting to undertake some task. This reminds the person concerned what was agreed. A simple example would be:

Action note (minute 234: financial management formula)

You will recall that you agreed at the last governor's meeting to write to the Chief Education Officer on behalf of the governors requesting him or his representative to meet a small deputation before the end of February if possible.

Governors' meetings, like those of any committee, can be tedious, interesting, pointless or fruitful. Given goodwill and a little ingenuity there is no reason why your own meetings should not be both satisfying and worthwhile. Governors have an important job to do, and if they can get the chemistry of their meetings right they are well on the way to doing it effectively.

Chapter 5

Life in school

'There's quite a lot of emphasis on environmental print in Year One.'

'We teach health education as a cross-curricular theme.'

'There is more time for options at Key Stage 4.'

At first glance the language of education can be baffling to lay people. Yet all fields of activity, whether they be hobbies like sailing, or professions like medicine, have developed their own terms. Most of the common expressions in education are clear and self-evident, and most teachers and heads, apart from one or two who have swallowed a dictionary of jargon, prefer to speak in plain English. In the above sentences 'environmental print' is the print that children see around when they are out and about, like DANGER or EXIT. A 'cross-curricular theme' is one that combines two or more subjects, like science, maths and English. 'Key Stage 4' is the fourth stage of the National Curriculum for pupils aged between 14 and 16.

We have often organised courses in which several governors have commented freely how ignorant they felt about what was happening in schools, and how much they welcomed the opportunity to hear an up-to-date account and be able to ask questions. 'I sit through meetings', said one parent governor, 'knowing little or nothing about several of the things we discuss.' Governors are usually reluctant to stop meetings so that someone can explain GCSE, profiling, the changing role of the LEA, or whatever.

Indeed several governors with long service on governing bodies or the Education Committee also confessed that, although they had picked up considerable information over the years, the world of education seemed to change so rapidly that it proved impossible for a lay person to keep abreast of recent developments.

Even professionals working in schools, teacher training, the inspectorate or advisory service find it difficult to maintain a firm grasp of all that is going on, but there are several sources of help available to both professionals and lay people. First of all many newspapers employ an education correspondent, and most of these, despite the occasional dud, perform a valuable service bringing stories about reports on education, new ideas in teaching or problems in schools to the attention of a wide readership. Popular magazines often feature educational topics or offer an advisory service.

Television and radio also report educational matters extensively, and programmes such as *Panorama*, *Horizon* and *World in Action* will often cover an issue in some depth with well filmed classroom scenes and usually, though not always, with a fair degree of objectivity. Many local and national radio programmes offer listeners a phone-in opportunity on educational matters from time to time, especially at the start of the school year during GCSE or A levels, or when a new educational initiative has been announced. It is worth watching some of the many programmes for teachers on new developments in schools or even occasionally sampling schools' television programmes or radio broadcasts, which frequently mirror the best of what is happening in primary and secondary schools.

A further source of information is to be found in the many reasonably priced paperbacks on education, some written especially for parents or anyone interested in schools. Alternatively, certain specialist magazines and periodicals appear regularly, and pamphlets are sometimes produced by various agencies, including the DFE and local authorities, to give a pithy digest of some important new development on current issues to the general public. A selection of these is given in the bibliography. You can also ask to see copies of the many circulars which are sent to schools.

Consequently this and the following chapter are only intended to give the reader a flavour of what is happening in primary and secondary schools, and to describe some of the issues and problems being faced by teachers and pupils. In view of the vastness of the area they can be but a starting point.

CHANGES IN SOCIETY

Many changes in school represent a response to changes in our society of which there have been many in recent times. Children leaving school in the last decade of the twentieth century will need more skills than any previous generation of pupils. There are several reasons for this.

One major reason is the disappearance of millions of unskilled jobs in the 1970s and 1980s. When we read about a multi-million pound investment scheme in industry it will usually obliterate unskilled jobs by the thousand. Tasks that were formerly undertaken by a large cohort of untrained and unskilled workers will in future be done by a small number of highly schooled technocrats, a squad of skilled and semi-skilled personnel, a sizeable group of bureaucrats responsible for paperwork, stock control, ordering and dispatching, and a tiny number of unskilled workers. The total workforce needed after the scheme is implemented will almost certainly be less overall than previously, and although some new posts will be created it is mostly the unskilled and semi-skilled ones which will disappear.

Secondly, it is the case that in adulthood generally more skills will be needed for family and community life as well as for work. Children currently at school will need to leave with considerable reading competence, a sound grasp of number, good social and communication skills, and a proper knowledge of where to find information and how to act on it in our increasingly complex, technological and bureaucratic society. Those who do not have these skills may find themselves unemployment casualties, or unable to sustain a satisfying adult life in the twenty-first century.

Many jobs which used to require very few basic skills now require a great deal more. Some, for example, need a higher reading age than formerly. 'Reading age' is a rough and ready concept to describe competence in reading. If someone has a reading age of 10 it means he reads like the average 10-year-old. Thus a 7-year-old with a reading age of 10 would be well ahead of his fellows, a 10-year-old would be about average, and a school leaver with a reading age of 10 would be severely handicapped in adult life, unable to take in anything other than simple texts such as are used by primary children. You need a reading age of about 15 or 16 to cope with this chapter. In other words average school leavers should be able to read it, even if they do not understand every word.

Shop stewards who used to negotiate orally now have to have a rudimentary knowledge of legislation covering matters such as unfair dismissals and safety at work. Much of the information about such Acts is written in quite complex language, and shop stewards with a very low reading age could not cope with the necessary reading, and would thus be unable to advise their colleagues appropriately.

A reading age of between 12 and 18 is required for various newspapers, and the mind-blowing complexity of some official forms is beyond the comprehension of most mortals, though this can be attributed to poor writing rather than to a defective human race. Similarly, although the mathematics of everyday life can be simple and repetitive, some of it is not so straightforward. Many quite ordinary people fill in income tax forms, pay interest on loans, run a household budget, make VAT returns or have to calculate speed, distance and cost when undertaking a journey. In some fields of work, such as engineering, the mathematical demands are far beyond what they were in the past.

A further aspect of modern life is the speed and scale of knowledge gathering. A doctor, scientist, teacher or someone working in business may be curious about research in their field of interest. They are often astonished to discover how many investigators have worked on the problem and written up their results in journals and books around the globe. One file of research in chemistry alone contains well over three million references, and computers must be used to search for relevant reports, the task now being beyond the human eye and hand. Every day thousands of further studies are added to these already vast repositories of information.

Teachers in school, therefore, realising that the extent of our knowledge on almost every subject prevents them from communicating all of it to the next generation of children, have to spend some time on basic skills and knowledge and the rest on equipping their pupils with the ability to find and use relevant information (see, for example, Figure 1).

Yet another change in society which affects schools is the rapid development of technology. Surgeons have had to learn about laser technology, and many of us had to come to grips with microcomputers and word processors. When hand-held calculators became available at reasonable prices, so that many children received them as presents and schools were able to contemplate purchasing sets of them, teachers faced a dilemma. Should they ignore the development and carry on as usual? Should they throw out most of their traditional numerical calculation work and just use calculators instead? Or should they give children an understanding of the relevant mathematics plus some practice in handworked solutions, and then show them how to use calculators to solve complex problems quickly and with understanding? Many teachers opted for the last solution.

A similar problem was faced when television appeared on a wide scale in almost every household. Some people saw it as a threat to human life, likely to produce a passive breed of spectator, and therefore not to be used in school, others felt it had exciting potential as an educational medium, capable of showing pupils a brilliantly performed Shakespeare play or an expensively produced film on volcanoes around the world such as no teacher could ever hope to make with limited resources.

Perhaps the most problematic aspect of all changes witnessed in our society in recent times is that it becomes increasingly difficult to predict what life will be like later in the twenty-first century, when children currently in school will be adults, many playing key roles in their community. Some forecasters predict a life of endless leisure, with the information technology revolution leading to automated factories and a minute workforce.

Others guess that the revolution will not so much abolish work, but rather lead to different kinds of jobs coming into existence. Just as people left the land to work in factories after the industrial revolution, so too they may leave factories to work in an enlarged leisure and recreational industry. As the factory machine became an extension of the human arm, so too the microprocessor might become an extension of the human brain, creating jobs and a life style we cannot accurately predict. If more people work in the leisure industry instead of factories, then social skills would be most important, as none of us wants to find our leisure soured by people who cannot get on with their fellows.

We may conclude, therefore, that schools have responded and must continue to respond to changes in society, whilst not always certain when and how change may come about. Increased demands for greater skill, for preparation, for community and family life and the world of work, for a quick response to technological innovation, for basic knowledge and strategies for

SUGAR & GROWTH OF A MOULD

Follow these instructions.

1 Copy these two diagrams into your book.
   If your book is plain paper, lay a sheet of lined paper under the page.

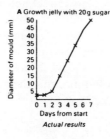

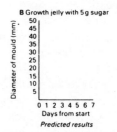

Answer these questions in sentences.

a Which experiment has most sugar in the growth jelly?

b Which of these three possibilities is the most likely? Give reasons for your answer.

   1 Mould A and mould B will grow in the same way.
   2 Mould A will grow faster than mould B.
   3 Mould B will grow faster than mould A.

c Which of these graphs best fits your answer to question b? Copy it on the graph B drawn in your book.

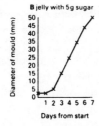

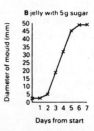

ASK YOUR TEACHER IF YOU SHOULD GO ON TO SHEET S5 OR E5

Figure 1 Pupils learn to find out for themselves: an experiment in growth
Source: *Science Watch*, P. Butler, D. Carrington, G. Ellis, Cambridge University Press, 1986

finding further information have led to several changes in primary and secondary schools, such as greater emphasis on vocational education for 14- to 18-year-olds, with better preparation for children for the world of work. It is to some of the questions about what and how we teach children in school that we now turn.

PRIMARY SCHOOLS

Primary education covers the 5 to 11 age range, and in some areas which have a first and middle school pattern, can include 12- year-olds. The 9 to 13 middle school is, for administrative purposes, regarded as a secondary school if most of its pupils are over 11.

Common arrangements of schools in the primary sector are shown below. Some schools have a nursery section for 3- to 5-year-olds attached to them.

1 Infant (5- to 7-year-olds) followed by junior (7- to 11-year-olds)
2 First (5- to 8-year-olds) followed by middle (8- to 12-year-olds)
3 First (5- to 9-year-olds) followed by middle (9- to 13-year-olds)

The idea of the primary school is that it lays the foundations for education by introducing children to important aspects of learning at a simple level, allowing this to be built upon at the secondary stage. Amongst the things to be learned will be important basic concepts in mathematics, science and humanities, and if all goes well there will be considerable development of children's language and ability to think. It is the time when children cover Key Stage 1 and Key Stage 2, the first two phases of the National Curriculum.

In view of the shortness of children's attention span at this age and the widely held view that they learn readily by doing something rather than being passive, there is usually some emphasis on so-called *activity methods*, which mean that children will be encouraged to discuss, explore and do, more frequently than look and listen. Thus those classrooms with rows of fixed desks, everyone facing the front and all doing the same task at the same time, so familiar in elementary schools earlier this century, have, in many schools, given way to small clusters of children seated around tables engaged in individual or group work, as well as whole class teaching.

Most primary schools are small, and this is reflected in numbers of the various types of schools in England. There are about four times as many primary schools as secondary schools, and the latter are often much bigger and more complex in organisation. Teachers usually take their own class for most of the day, whereas in secondary schools each subject may be taught by a different specialist. In recent years there has been some movement towards a degree of specialisation in the primary school, and it is now more common for teachers to swap classes occasionally with another teacher so that each can give expert help to more than one group in music, design & technology, number work, language or whatever happens to be their particular interest or specialism.

Buildings are of all shapes and sizes. Although most have been purpose-built in the post-war era, there are many older, primary schools, some built in the nineteenth century, with solid walls, high windows and cramped classrooms. In more recent times school buildings have more window space, better lighting and ventilation, and are frequently flexible in design, allowing spaces to be used in different ways. There has been considerable use of transportable classrooms which can be set down temporarily in the grounds of a school with increasing numbers, and moved subsequently elsewhere if necessary. In some older schools the 'temporary' buildings erected in the 1930s and 1940s still stand, apparently defying all attempts to have them demolished.

Open plan primary schools have few interior walls and can be used in a variety of ways. Many were built in the late 1960s and 1970s and were meant to suit the preferred style of teachers who found themselves spilling out into the corridors of traditional schools. Sometimes there are two or three large units within the school, each containing perhaps 100 or so pupils with three or four teachers. The teachers may work as a team or separately. The open plan area will be divided up into various sections, subdivided perhaps by bookshelves, cupboards or sliding screens, one part carpeted, another with a vinyl floor covering, depending on the type of activity undertaken there. One area may have books, cassette recorders and headphones, to be used principally for reading and language work. Another part may contain maths books and equipment. A sink and Formica topped surface may be found in another area, and children will don their aprons and paint, glue and make things there. There may be a 'quiet corner', a little ante-room where children can read on their own, and for music or noisy activities there will probably be a sound-proofed conventional box classroom so no one else will be disturbed.

A pupil working in such a school may start a project in the language area, move later to library and resources, go on to the 'messy area' to construct something, retire to the quiet corner for reflection and return to a table elsewhere to finish off. Teachers may be stationed in language or number areas, move freely around answering questions, checking progress and encouraging children, or work with a particular group of children in a certain topic in the more conventional one teacher/one class situation. There are many ways of working in open plan schools and teachers' views about such schools vary considerably, from enthusiastic support to great dislike. Similarly the buildings are different, some brilliant in design, others noisy and badly conceived.

SECONDARY SCHOOLS

Before the second world war over 90 per cent of children aged 5 to 14 were educated in all-age elementary schools, and the idea of secondary education for all was a dream. After the war the common pattern was for children to be selected at the age of 10 or 11 for either a grammar school or a secondary modern. Provision varied according to the area in which children lived, and it was not unknown for 15 per cent of children to go to grammar schools in one area and 20 per cent in a nearby authority. Over the nation as a whole the range was wider still.

In certain parts of the country, notably London, there already existed comprehensive schools taking children of all abilities, and in 1965 the Labour government of the time issued a circular requesting local education authorities to submit plans for reorganising secondary education in their area on comprehensive lines. Several schemes were approved, and most local authorities opted to open some new schools and make the best use of existing buildings rather than underwrite the vast capital expenditure which would result from a total rebuilding programme. This often explains why some schools have two or more sites. Perhaps twenty or thirty years earlier a girls' school and a boys' school were merged, or a grammar and secondary modern school were joined together.

Amongst schemes adopted were the following, in some cases in modified form:

1 all-through comprehensive (11- to 18-year-olds)
2 junior comprehensive (11–14), senior comprehensive (14–18)
3 junior comprehensive (11–16), senior comprehensive for those wishing to transfer at 13 and stay on after the minimum school-leaving age (13–18)
4 junior comprehensive (11–16), sixth form or tertiary college (16+)
5 middle school (9–13), senior comprehensive (13–18)

Consequently the 1970s saw considerable changes in secondary schools on a scale never experienced before. Not only did many schools reorganise, but at the same time the school-leaving age was raised to 16, there were increased problems of discipline, especially in inner-city areas, and schools often became bigger and more complex.

Since teachers now had to deal with the whole ability range in the same school, many new books and curriculum packages were produced locally or nationally, and different forms of grouping were tried as they strove to find the fairest and most effective ways of teaching. Teachers who had never before taught the brightest pupils and those who had never previously worked with average and slow learners had to develop new professional skills to be able to teach across the whole ability range. Sadly, this period coincided with a spell of financial stringency, and most teachers, unable to obtain any release of time to study, plan and reflect, had to acquire these skills on the job.

Nowadays the secondary years are when the 3rd and 4th Key Stages of the National Curriculum are covered. Pupils take ten subjects, plus religious education and, in Wales, the study of Welsh. It is also the period when they take their first significant public examination like GCSE, A levels and the many vocational qualifications which can now be taught in schools as well as colleges of higher education.

Secondary school buildings are as different from one another as are primary school buildings. In many local authorities substantial secondary school building programmes have been undertaken during recent years. Some of these have been quite exciting multi-purpose buildings, having leisure centres, libraries, arts centres or a theatre attached to them, thus offering a superb set of facilities to the whole community. There are places where a stranger looking for the school is advised to follow the road signs marked 'Sports forum', and when he arrives he finds an unusual restriction forbidding street car parking during evenings and at weekends, simply because the facilities are almost as widely used at those times as they are during the day.

During the 1980s many local authorities opted for a tertiary college form of reorganization for pupils between 16 and 19. The advantage was that wide choices could be offered, not only A levels but vocational awards such as those offered by the Business and Technician Educational Council (BTEC) or the City and Guilds of London Institute (CGLI). The disadvantage was that younger pupils in the 11–16 or 12–16 feeder secondary schools lost the benefit of having senior pupils in their school.

TEACHERS AND TEACHING

There are well over 400,000 teachers in England and Wales, and currently people can train for teaching predominantly via two different routes. The first pattern is for 18-year-olds to spend three or four years at a university or college. During their course they study specialised subjects and learn how to teach at the same time. This is called the *concurrent pattern* and students may be required to do teaching practice at any stage of their course. They will usually leave with a BEd or BA (Ed.) degree.

The second pattern is for would-be teachers to take their first degree at a university or college. Having obtained usually a BA or BSc entirely devoted to the study of a single academic subject, such as French or physics or some combination of academic subjects, but not containing any teaching practice or study of education, they will go on to spend a concentrated year devoted entirely to teacher training, at the end of which they obtain their licence to teach, the Postgraduate Certificate in Education. This is known as the *consecutive* pattern.

Until the 1970s it was generally the case that BA and BSc graduates were trained entirely in universities, and non-graduates and BEd graduates in colleges of education. Since then the situation has been much more fluid, and each pattern of training can be found in many different higher education situations, though some aspects of the previous system survive. In 1989 the government introduced a *licensed teacher scheme* which allowed mature entrants with industrial or commercial experience to enter teaching with on-the-job training. Governors may acquire some excellent recruits through this route, but it is crucial for proper training to be given, otherwise, unsuitable people could create mayhem in the classroom.

During the early 1990s the government sought to broaden the means of getting into the teaching profession, as well as to give more emphasis to school-based teacher training. One of the concerns expressed by governors at the shift to more school-based teacher training is that it may take away some of their best teachers to work with students, or that pupils may have too many student teachers. The next generation has to be trained somewhere, and no one wants to involve teachers who have no understanding of the realities of classroom life. However, the best training schemes are usually based on an equal partnership between schools and training institutions. There may be major problems recruiting sufficient teachers during the 1990s, as many retirements take place, and every effort will have to be made to widen the recruitment base, especially by attracting people who have good relevant experience.

It is important not to be misled by graduate status: many non-graduates are outstanding teachers who never had the opportunity to take a degree, and who would probably have been the stars of their BEd or BA/BSc class had they had the opportunity. Indeed a large number of the most successful Open University graduates were formerly non-graduate teachers, and other teachers have gone on to take a degree from a university or college during their teaching career as mature, in-service students.

Once teachers have qualified there are several forms of in-service work they can undertake. During the 1980s there was a considerable shift to school-based courses for teachers. The teachers' contract allows for five days each year, sometimes referred to as 'Baker days', after the minister who introduced them, when pupils are not in school but teachers are, which can be used for such purposes. Universities, colleges, local education authorities, teachers' centres, the DES, and a number of other bodies all provide courses for short or long duration.

Teachers can attend anything from one-hour sessions or half-day workshops up to a whole-week, one-term or even to a course covering up to a couple of years, the longer ones leading to further professional qualifications like advanced diplomas or master's degrees. Release from school and secondment on salary became rare in the 1980s and 1990s, and teachers are usually delighted to have governors' support for in-service training. Although many teachers have been frustrated by wishing to attend courses and not being able to, there is the equally important problem of the teacher who would benefit from in-service work but chooses not to take advantage of it.

The school-based or school-focused programme allows teachers to improvise something they feel is of use to their community and draw in outsiders as necessary. There are several examples of governors attending parts or the whole of such courses and finding the experience extremely valuable. A

RESOURCES FOR LEARNING

9.00 a.m. *Introduction: recent developments in resource-based learning*
Mr. J. Brown, Senior Adviser, Exchester

9.45   *Adapting and extending the traditional school library*
Mrs A. Johnson, Head of Exchester West Comprehensive School

10.30   Coffee

10.45   Discussion in departmental groups of implications for various subjects

12.00 p.m. Plenary session

12.30   Lunch

1.30   *How children learn from various media*
Dr C. Smith, Dept of Education, Exchester University

2.15   Practical sessions, each member of staff to join one group

A	Making self-study kits	Dr Smith
B	Microcomputer software	Mrs Johnson
C	Assembling sets of newspaper cuttings and archives	Mrs B. Phillips (Head of History)
D	Making and using television material	Mrs L. Thomas (Head of Biology)
E	Interactive technology	Mrs D. Naylor (Head of Media Studies) Exchester South Comprehensive School

3.45   Plenary session

---

typical programme for a one-day, school-based in-service course, with a mixture of home talent and visiting speakers, is shown in the box above.

Teaching is a very busy job. Some studies of teachers have shown that they engage in as many as 1000 contacts with children in a day, when they ask or are asked questions, praise or reprimand, assign tasks, or respond to demands on their attention. This busy professional life style can extend over the whole year, making 5000 such contacts a week and several millions in a whole career. Put another way, imagine tapping your pet tortoise on its shell every four seconds. The effect on its nervous system would be considerable, the RSPCA would soon pay you a call, and no doubt the tortoise would be pressing the governors for some shell-based in-service work.

In addition, teachers nowadays fill many roles. In some schools they even find themselves acting as front-line social workers, the first to see a bruised child or hear a family hard-luck story. Below are but some of the roles which teachers may find themselves filling at some time during their teaching a busy professional week.

- *Expert.* Helping children learn information, or knowing where to find it in various subject areas, answering children's questions.
- *Counsellor.* Advising pupils about careers, personal problems, important decisions.
- *Social worker.* Dealing with problem families, children from broken homes, liaising with various social services.
- *Parent.* Acting as substitute mother or father.
- *Jailer.* Coping with pupils who would prefer not to be at school, dealing with truants.
- *Bureaucrat.* Filling in registers, forms, returns or orders.
- *Public relations officer.* Explaining to parents what the school is doing, dealing with local radio and newspapers.
- *Assessor.* Marking books, grading tests, devising and administering examinations, writing references.
- *Technician.* Assembling or dismantling equipment.
- *Manager.* Making decisions about the most effective use of available resources.

It is because teaching is an exacting job, and because most teachers are committed to their work, that the occasional teacher who is incompetent becomes conspicuous.

The 1986 Education Act introduced the whole question of teacher appraisal, which is required by law, though it is left to schools to decide how it should be done, under the supervision of their LEA. There are many ways of appraising teachers and most teachers themselves like to place the emphasis on helping them improve their professional skills, rather than merely earning a mark out of ten. During their appraisal teachers must be observed teaching by their appraiser, usually a more senior teacher in the school. They also need to decide what aspect of their teaching they will focus on, perhaps class management, or developing small group work, which they must try to implement over coming years. This can produce a request for in-service, to help improve what they do and meet their targets.

Any parent will confirm that children who like their teachers skip happily to school, and those who do not have to be cajoled into attending. Teachers themselves are very embarrassed to find as a colleague one of the small number of ill-suited or inept practitioners, and, contrary to popular belief, teachers do not have a licence to teach for life, come what may. Amongst the more thorny problems which may surface at governors' meetings will be found that of the teacher about whom there are serious complaints.

There is not a professional code of conduct which, if broken, leads to teachers being 'struck off the list' or disbarred in quite the same way as happens in the medical and legal professions. On the other hand the procedure is not radically different. If a teacher commits a criminal offence, or is guilty of serious misconduct, he will be asked to appear before the local authority's disciplinary committee or its equivalent, and he may lose his job. Furthermore, the Home Office reports all serious convictions of teachers to the Secretary of State who, after giving the teacher an opportunity to make representations, may order that the person be no longer employed as a teacher (car parking offences are not reported!). Such blacklisted teachers may not be employed elsewhere without having been reinstated by the DFE. (The blacklist is officially known as 'List 99'.)

The incompetent rather than criminal teacher is a different matter – though he too is liable to dismissal. Usually heads of department and heads of schools, aided by external advisers, will make exhaustive attempts to help someone in this position. If, however, people are satisfied that all help has failed or been rejected then, provided proper warnings have been issued and proper channels gone through, this teacher too can lose his job. What has been said above applies equally to heads. The reason that a certain popular belief persists that the teachers or heads cannot be shown the door is that the process is rightly longwinded and is not undertaken lightly. Certainly in any school which has a dismissal case the governors will find it figures high and frequently on their agenda.

We have spent some time on the question of incompetent or malevolent teachers only because when they are encountered they cause the greatest distress to their pupils, their colleagues and the authorities. It must be stressed that this is a small, if problematic, section of the community, most of whom are highly professional in their job.

CURRICULUM

The knowledge explosion and changes in society have put immense pressure on the curriculum. Consider these short extracts from history and geography textbooks written in the 1870s when pupils had to learn off by heart a set of packaged answers and repeat these like a catechism. They reflect the society of their day, when an uneducated peasantry received its first compulsory education at the hands of untrained teachers handling large classes. Life in family and society was stern, children were to be seen and not heard, and unquestioning obedience was encouraged and valued.

Q: Who was Henry VIII?
A: Son of Henry VII.
Q: What was his character?
A: As a young man, he was bluff, generous, right royal, and very handsome.
Q: How was he when he grew older?
A: He was bloated, vain, cruel and selfish.
Q: What is the climate of England?
A: Moist, but healthy.
Q: What is the character of the English people?
A: Brave, intelligent and very persevering.
Q: What is the size of England?
A: About 430 miles long and 320 broad.

During the twentieth century children have been encouraged to assume a less subservient role, a great deal has been discovered about how people learn and fail to learn, and it is likely that the style of much of what is taught in the curriculum in modern schools is to offer pupils more opportunity for individual thought than did old textbooks. On the other hand one will still see mechanical and senseless rote learning at all levels, and some critics feel there has been too little movement away from authoritarian teacher-directed learning.

The National Curriculum

For most of the twentieth century England and Wales were unique in Europe in leaving individual schools to fashion their own curriculum. The 1988 Education Act established a National Curriculum, common elsewhere. The National Curriculum consists of *core* subjects: mathematics, English and science (plus Welsh in Welsh speaking schools); and *foundation subjects* – (a) history, geography, technology, music, art and physical education (plus Welsh in areas where Welsh is not spoken), (b) a modern foreign language (secondary pupils only). Religious education has been legally required since the 1944 Education Act.

Over the years there have been many bodies responsible for curriculum and assessment matters. Sometimes there have been two separate bodies but at other times just a single organisation. After the 1988 Education Act there were two official councils, one for curriculum, the other for testing, but in 1993 these were merged in a single body, the Schools Curriculum and Assessment Authority (SCAA). Part of its duties is to oversee the National Curriculum and the testing of pupils at the end of each Key Stage, when children are 7, 11, 14 or 16.

Test results will be made available to governors, the LEA and parents, as mentioned in Chapter 2, and governors must keep these under review. There is some latitude within the National Curriculum, because the government, though it has prescribed the subjects, does not specify how these should be taught. Heads, teachers and governors should, therefore, still be able to create some flexibility with a little imagination. Nor is it essential for every aspect of the National Curriculum to be taught as a single subject. Technology, for example, will occur in more than one field, and the well-established traditions of project and topic work in primary schools, described below, allow for subjects such as geography and history to be taught under themes like 'canals' or 'our village'.

There has been some concern that national tests, especially for 7-year-olds, produce a high level of anxiety, and it is up to governors to monitor this by keeping in touch with parents. National tests should, in any case, only be a part of a school's assessment programme. Many teachers make regular use of short tests and the national tests every four years or so ought not to be allowed to dominate what is taught in school.

One matter certain to be of interest to governors is the publication of schools' test scores in an authority or region in 'league table' form. Crude comparisons tell us little about the quality of teaching in a school. For example, a school in a socially deprived area is likely to score below a school in a socially privileged part of town, not necessarily because the teaching is poor, but rather because the school's intake is of lower intellectual ability. If Liverpool Football Club played the Little Piddlington Cubs at football and won by eight goals to nil that could actually represent a triumph for the Cubs and a poor display for the professionals. League tables of schools' exam scores must be treated with the same degree of caution and background factors taken into account, otherwise much unjustified misery, or complacency, will ensue.

PRIMARY SCHOOL CURRICULUM

Primary schools operate various patterns. Some follow a timetable of thirty- or forty-minute lessons, sometimes with the 'basics' in the morning and art, craft, music and project work in the afternoon. Others have what is known as the *integrated day*, which may be based on no timetable of subjects at all but allow teachers and pupils to spend the day on a variety of individual and group work. Teachers who operate the integrated approach successfully have to prepare skilfully, and record progress meticulously. Usually each child has a certain set of assignments which must be completed, some mathematics, some reading, some written work, and then a topic, often based on guided choice. At its best the system allows a child to pursue each task in his own time and not have to break off at some inappropriate point.

Well organised primary classrooms are a joy to see, there being an air of busy enjoyment around the place. Badly organised classrooms have children wasting time, spending days over unexacting tasks, and learning little. A typical daily record of four children from a class taught along integrated lines might look as shown in the box below, a tick denoting that the teacher had checked progress in the area.

	Number	Daily diary	Project (personal)	Project (class)	Art/ craft	Reading	Comment
Mary	✓	✓	✓		✓	✓	Now understands fractions very well.
John	✓	✓		✓		✓	Moved to red readers but found it hard going.
Colin	✓	✓	✓	✓		✓	
Alice	✓	✓		✓		✓	Beginning to lose interest in water project, must switch tomorrow.

Reading

There are hundreds of well produced reading books suitable for children, some graded for beginners, others beautifully illustrated and in appropriate language for children who have learned to read a little and need to become more proficient through enjoying reading.

Several methods of teaching reading have been in and out of vogue in recent years:

1 *Phonics.* This is the best-known traditional method, and involves the pupil in learning to recognise individual letters and sounds and then blend them into the whole word: d – o – g equals dog. It is more confusing when words like bough, cough, through and iron are encountered, but it is vital for children to learn the sounds of letters nonetheless.

2 *Look and say/whole word.* This is a method whereby pupils learn the whole word as a shape or pattern. The teacher often uses pictures and flashcards at the outset, so that a child might learn to recognise even a complex word

like 'television' quite early on. The advantage of this method is that reading matter can be made more interesting, involving sentences like 'John liked watching television' rather than 'The cat sat on the mat.' One disadvantage is that children sometimes fail to distinguish accurately the components of longer words and see, for example, 'television' as tel- followed by a jumble of letters. They might therefore read 'telephone', 'telegram' or even 'telxyzzzon' as 'television'. Thus many teachers prefer to use some combination of whole word reading and phonics in their teaching of reading.

3 *Sentence/language experience*. Another approach tries to integrate reading and writing rather than teach them separately. For example, the *Breakthrough to Literacy* project provides children with a simple aid to sentence writing. Some 200 or so high frequency words are already printed on separate plastic strips and the child can add words of his own on blanks. Children can write their own sentences by assembling a mixture of printed words and their own choices in the Sentence Maker.

4 *Real books*. Some teachers believe that children learn to read best by being immersed in 'real' books, not a reading scheme. The advantage is that 'real' books, that is, the sort of books that are simply written for children to read, often have good stories and natural language. The disadvantage is that children may not actively learn the structure of language properly.

Few teachers adhere rigidly to one mode of teaching reading, and most will exploit some combination of methods and use carefully graded reading schemes, which take children from beginner to fluent reader, alongside suitable children's fiction and books of general interest.

What is often neglected, however, is some work on the higher skills of reading. Once a child can read with a fair degree of confidence he needs to learn the kind of reading skills essential in much of adolescent and adult life. These skills involve the ability to scan or skim, read rapidly, to slow down and read over again a difficult passage, to use a book index or library catalogue, to make notes summarising sections or recording key points, to discriminate between styles of writing, and to recognise fact from opinion.

Some reading schemes, like *Flying Boot* (see Figure 2), try to combine the best of the various approaches, as most teachers prefer mixed methods anyway, as well as capitalise on the natural print in the environment (like shop signs, warning notices, etc).

Writing

Before the typewriter, having a 'fair hand' was an important selling point in the job market and a valued attribute in Victorian society, when clerks painstakingly entered pages of beautifully scripted entries into huge ledgers. Today, although good handwriting is still cultivated in most schools, there is

Figure 2 A mixed approach to reading, using phonics, natural language and print from the environment
Source: *Flying Boot*, Ted Wragg, Thomas Nelson, 1994

also considerable attention devoted to what children write as well as how they write it. Teaching young children how to write involves their learning in the first instance how to hold the pen or pencil, form letters and write from left to right. They are usually taught the small letters first and capitals later, and normally learn to print first using simple traditional letter forms or one of the italic styles.

We use writing in many contexts and for many purposes in our ordinary lives, so children will learn to write for different audiences. Once having mastered the act of writing they will write stories, accounts of their experiences and reports of work undertaken. Both 'handwriting' and the need to write good English in a variety of circumstances are an important part of the National Curriculum. Also children are expected to learn to use a word processor to draft and re-draft a piece of writing until it is the best they can produce.

The term 'creative writing' has been frequently used in recent years. For some it represented the best in the so-called primary school revolution, after which children were encouraged to express themselves in their own way, rather than ape the writings and views of their elders. To the critics it was a sloppy 'anything goes' notion likely to be full of wrong spellings ignored by the teacher afraid to dampen emergent genius. As ever the reality was that few teachers conformed to either stereotype. Most sought to achieve some spontaneity from their pupils, and corrected spellings and punctuation judiciously, neither condoning errors nor fuming with rage at a missing apostrophe.

Analysis of a primary school child's day might show her writing a diary entry, a letter, a note to a friend, an account of a school trip, a made-up story, copying from a book or blackboard, describing the weather, and compiling a shopping list, all during the one period of twenty-four hours. Many children in school will write more and for a wider range of purposes than their parents. When the quality of children's writing is poor it is either because they have been given little practice, or because too much of what they write is mechanically copied from books, the blackboard or worksheets.

Mathematics

There is a great deal of talk about 'old' and 'new' mathematics, which often annoys mathematicians, who find nothing 'new' about so-called new maths. It has always been there, they argue, it simply was not being taught in most schools. Recent primary school mathematics teaching has tried to get away from mechanical learning and endless repetition, and move towards letting children understand the mathematics they learn. Children will learn not simply that $5 \times 4 = 20$, but that 5×4 is also the same as 4×5 or 10×2 or $5 + 5 + 5 + 5$ or $(3 \times 5) + 5$. They will learn about shapes and get the feel of their properties by making and extending various shapes, rotating or classifying them. They will also learn the measurement of time, length and mass (see Figure 3).

In general they will learn better at primary age by directly experiencing mathematics, so that much of the work will be practical, using blocks, counters and other equipment as necessary, or involving children in considering aspects of their immediate environment, like measuring the volume of their classroom, the height of their friends, or what they can do in a minute, or finding circle and triangle shapes encountered in everyday life.

Some of the debate about primary school mathematics centres around the teaching of tables, and adults often fantasise that they were themselves mathematical wizards at an early age because they can still chant a nine times table. Critics of primary maths teaching complain that some pupils have to work out 9 × 8 by writing out the number 8 nine times and adding it all up. Skilful primary school teachers recognise that both an intuitive understanding of mathematics and, on occasion, a speedy and accurate response are required, and prepare children for several eventualities, without either boring them to death with mindless repetition or failing to drive it all home after the experience and discovery phase.

Science

Before the National Curriculum was introduced in the late 1980s various surveys were very critical of primary science teaching. Some children appeared to be learning nothing at all about science until they reached secondary school, and only a small number of teachers appeared to be doing worthwhile and exciting work. Yet children at primary school age are immensely curious about their surroundings, and it is a great pity that few teachers preparing to teach the under-11s had any significant science course in their training until recent times.

A great deal of science can be learned from the immediate environment, and children of 3 or 4 often ask important scientific questions. Below are just seven of the thousands of questions children ask their teachers or parents which can lead on to simple work in science or technology. All of them relate to topics in the National Curriculum.

- Why do germs make you ill?
- Why do things fall when you drop them?
- Where do birds go in winter?
- Why do we need oil?
- Why am I out of breath when I run fast?
- What is electricity and why can it kill you?
- How does a calculator do sums so quickly?

Skilful teachers use every opportunity to engage children's interest in science. Many toys can be used to investigate basic scientific principles, for example

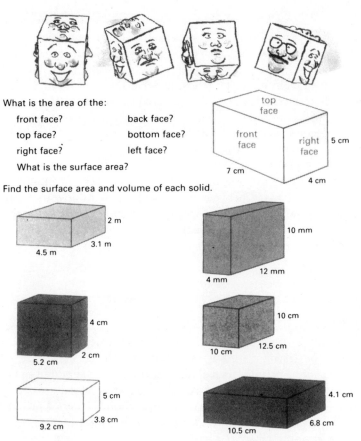

What is the area of the:

front face?   back face?
top face?   bottom face?
right face?   left face?

What is the surface area?

Find the surface area and volume of each solid.

Get a rectangular box. Measure its length, width, and height to the nearest centimetre.
Calculate its surface area and volume.

Determine the surface area and volume of your classroom.

Figure 3 A page from *Ginn Mathematics 6+*, Textbook 3, for older primary pupils (1992)

how high a ball bounces on wood, carpet, polystyrene or water. The working of the human body is of concern to children and early health education can deal with tooth decay, a balanced diet or pollution. Elastic bands, lollipop sticks and construction toys can be useful for elementary education in technology.

It is vital for all adults to show an interest in and be knowledgeable about science and technology, and primary school governors should take an interest in what is being done in this area of primary school life as well as the three Rs. It should be remembered, however, that although some primary schools may set aside time for science on a timetable, others may choose to teach science as part of an integrated approach via project work.

SECONDARY SCHOOL CURRICULUM

The secondary school curriculum is too vast to describe in a short space, and much of what has been said about primary schools above applies to the secondary sector. In some schools brand new subjects have appeared which may not be familiar to parents' and grandparents' generation, or they may be contemporary versions of lessons formerly under a different name. For example, in New York drugs education had to become a major concern at both elementary and high school level, because so many children were dying from using heroin or one of the lethal drugs, or were seriously injuring their health, and parents themselves, never having been taught at school about the effects of various drugs, were clamouring for informed advice to be given to children in good time. There is a pressing concern in the UK nowadays about drugs education and the need for children to understand the dangers of glue sniffing, or about learning the nature of AIDS.

Technology in schools nowadays is not just a matter of learning a bit of electricity, woodwork or circuitry. The National Curriculum does contain elements from traditional woodwork and metalwork lessons, but also includes leather, ceramics, plastics and textiles, and involves the use of modern power-tools and machinery, as well as traditional craftsmanship. It also includes cookery and home economics.

It would take several books to describe all that is happening in secondary schools, so a brief description of certain developments will suffice. As in primary school teaching there has been emphasis in certain secondary school science curricula on discovery learning. Great scientists devise theories which they then put to the test. If successive carefully controlled experiments produce the same findings the theory is upheld. Thus pupils may speculate about what will happen if a current from batteries is passed through different materials. Various experiments will be conducted by groups to test out their 'hypotheses'. Finally a principle will be extracted from the results and compared with the textbook versions of scientific laws (see Figure 4).

In foreign language teaching there has been some movement towards

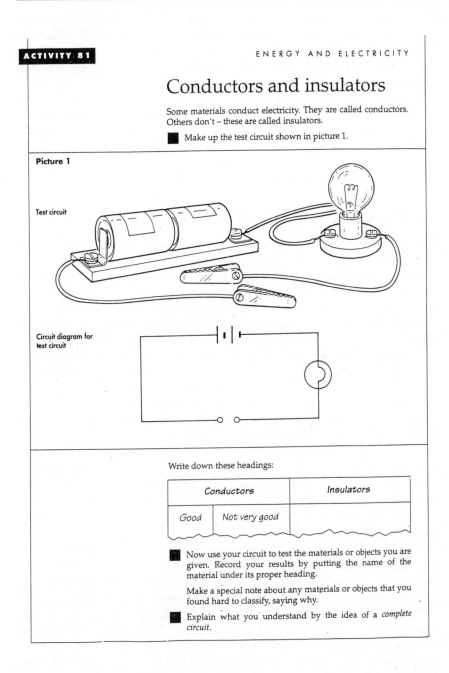

ACTIVITY 81

ENERGY AND ELECTRICITY

Conductors and insulators

Some materials conduct electricity. They are called conductors.
Others don't – these are called insulators.

■ Make up the test circuit shown in picture 1.

Picture 1

Test circuit

Circuit diagram for
test circuit

Write down these headings:

Conductors		Insulators
Good	Not very good	

■ Now use your circuit to test the materials or objects you are given. Record your results by putting the name of the material under its proper heading.

Make a special note about any materials or objects that you found hard to classify, saying why.

■ Explain what you understand by the idea of a *complete circuit*.

Figure 4 Pupils study conductors and insulators
Source: *Science World: Teacher's Resource Book 2*, edited by J. Holman, Thomas Nelson, 1994

stressing oral competence. Instead of the turgid grammar-bound books of yesteryear based on the traditions of Latin teaching, a modern language teacher today may choose from a vast selection of books, flashcards, filmstrips, tapes and audio-visual courses which make use of sound and video tapes of native speakers and pictures of scenes in the country whose language is being studied. Some schools have had language laboratories installed which offer each pupil a booth containing a tape recorder, whilst the teacher sits at a console and is able to monitor individuals or talk to the whole class. Many courses currently on the market stress everyday life in the country being studied, and children learn the conversation necessary for shopping, travel, family life and leisure (see Figure 5).

English teaching in secondary schools has become very broad, and English teachers may find themselves doing a wide range of children's fiction and adult literature, creative writing, drama, developing oral skills and self-confidence and a host of other assignments. There has been emphasis on every teacher being responsible for teaching language, on the grounds that it is better for a physics or maths teacher to explain what 'inversely proportional' means when it occurs in a lesson, rather than to opt out, claiming that the English teacher will have to deal with it one day. Nevertheless a great deal of responsibility for language development still does fall on the shoulders of English teachers.

For several years there was a tendency for some English teachers to react vigorously against language work, partly because of the tedious emphasis on clause analysis, punctuation and spelling, which had made English lessons unpopular in many secondary schools. More English teachers now try to teach the higher skills of reading and attempt to sensitise children to the effects of various language choices. For example, a class may study several letters sent to a person, some pompous, some longwinded, some flippant, some insulting, and discover how words are used to convey messages and what impact they have on the recipient (see, for example, Figure 6). Similarly they may study different accounts of the same political, social or sporting occasion in a number of newspapers to see how writers of various persuasions describe the same events.

Other subjects too have seen changes or pressure for more to be included in their syllabus. Pupils studying history or geography may do their own survey work, consulting archives and old newspapers, interviewing local farmers or shopkeepers, going on field trips to see industrial archaeology or geographical features. Local history and geography may figure prominently in the early stages of secondary schools, and urban geography – the study of housing, roadways, the location of precincts, factories and supermarkets – has become a legitimate part of some pupils' lessons.

Religious education has often been widened in multi-ethnic schools to include a comparative study of other religious beliefs, or sometimes to include moral education in an attempt to equip children with a sense of right and

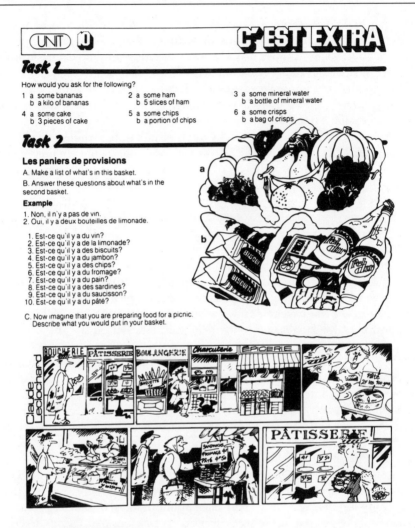

Figure 5 An extract from *Tricolore* 1b
Source: *Tricolore*, Stage One, Pupils' Book 1B, Sylvia Honnor, Ron Holt and Heather Mascie-Taylor, E.J. Arnold, 1980

wrong. For other teachers religious education remains exclusively the study of Christianity. Some forms of RE syllabus have been very wide indeed, including several world religions and even permitting reference to communism, always guaranteed to provoke a burst of letters when announced in the press. The law now requires religious education to cover both Christianity and one world religion, through Christianity should receive major attention.

In addition to what might be called 'traditional' secondary school subjects there are several 'cross-curricular themes' which embrace two or more subjects, or exist in their own right.

Figure 6 Children learn the importance of emphasis and voice intonation in communication
Source: *Your Language Two*. Maura Healy, Macmillan, London and Basingstoke, 1981

Humanities/social studies

Often this combines geography, history and perhaps another subject. Pupils may study a theme like 'transport', 'housing', 'society', 'machines and our lives' with reference to our own and other societies, including primitive tribes. Although several commercially produced courses exist many teachers have worked together to improvise their own.

Media studies

Children will spend hours of their lives watching television, yet until recently almost nothing was done in school to encourage discrimination. Television in particular, radio and newspapers to a lesser degree, inform and shape children's attitudes to a variety of issues, offer heroes and villains and influence their money spending and leisure habits. A media studies course might involve pupils in learning how to make television and radio programmes, understanding how news programmes or newspapers are put together, learning the tricks used by advertisers and politicians to persuade buyers or voters, analysing popular entertainment shows, and seeing how important mass media are in our daily lives. Media studies are often part of an English or humanities programme.

Political education

The 1986 Education Act ruled out political indoctrination; not that much of that actually occurred. Most people advocating some systematic teaching about politics do not indoctrinate but rather look at politics as the use of power in any society including our own. Thus how decisions are made locally, nationally or internationally is of central interest, and party politics is but one part of this concern. In a true democracy, it is argued, adults must understand the decision-making process. Rather than listen to tedious lectures about Parliament or what the council tax is, pupils may well simulate some local problem, where to build a shopping centre or a motorway, and role play the various parties involved as money is raised, plans devised, votes cast and objections heard. Pupil observers are receiving political education by attending governors' meetings.

Personal, social and moral education (PSME)

In some schools departments called 'Personal relationships' have been established and PSME is built into the timetable. In others it is not formally scheduled and taught, but is part of what is sometimes called the 'hidden curriculum', a phrase devised to describe the many things schools teach and children learn which are not officially on the timetable of lessons. For example, if one feels a sense of lurking violence on the premises of a particular school, the building is vandalised, pupils barged out of the way along corridors, wall displays tatty, crumbling and defaced and no one apparently cares, there seems to be a powerful message that human beings do not count, that disorder is acceptable and that concern for others is not to be encouraged. If, on the other hand, the school clearly is concerned about the welfare of its members, that children are not bullied, that those of modest ability are not scoffed at, that privacy can be respected or that a craftsman's pride in collective achievement is permissible, then important social education is taking place every time an insensitive pupil is counselled.

Health education

Doctors tell us that adults are often astonishingly ill-informed about the workings of their own body, pregnant mothers unaware that smoking may cause smaller babies, and, worse, obese middle-aged men ignorant of the consequences of lack of exercise, drinkers not knowledgeable about the effects on the body's vital organs of excessive alcohol, and people on high dosages of amphetamines or barbiturates apparently not realising they have a problem. Some interesting work on all aspects of health education is being undertaken in many schools nowadays, and whilst information alone will not necessarily prevent abuse of the human body, it may help in those cases where people might unwittingly do themselves a mischief through their own ignorance.

Technical and vocational education

In response to the concerns about school leavers who were not prepared for the world of work, there were experimental schemes in technical and vocational education for 14- to 18-year-olds throughout the 1980s. Pupils studied and acquired work experience in various fields, such as microtechnology, the caring professions (e.g. nursing and social work), the built environment (jobs in the building trade), to help them understand the range of jobs they might one day do and appreciate which qualities they would need to develop.

After initial pilot experiments the scheme spread to most schools. The emphasis was on learning by direct experience, and pupils were encouraged to negotiate much more for themselves than had previously been the case. Many pupils took formal qualifications as part of their course, and some obtained the Certificate in Prevocational Education (CPVE) at the age of 17 or so. For many years schools were not permitted to offer certain vocational qualifications, but they may now do so. This has been particularly welcomed in rural areas where there is no college of further education and where the school can give pupils a valuable start in some vocational field.

We have several times apologised for the inadequacy of the brief description of some of the recent developments which affect life in school. Inevitably any attempt to encapsulate the vast complexity of what happens in the lessons of over 400,000 teachers in a single chapter must omit a great deal. It would also be wrong to pretend that all the recent developments described above take place in our schools. There are schools which have never changed for years, despite the advent of the National Curriculum, and others which have seen innovation without change (i.e. the introduction of some new curriculum package but with the same strategies used beforehand). Many schools, however, have been dizzy with the whirligig of new courses, changes in organisation and changes in personnel.

Nor would it be correct to say that new ideas invariably ensure outstanding success. We have both in our travels round schools seen language courses where the children senselessly and uncomprehendingly chanted German phrases over and over again like reluctant conscripts to some junior Nuremberg rally.

Nevertheless, despite some poor schools and inadequate teachers, it is our view that the majority of teachers in both primary and secondary schools have spent a great deal of time and effort attempting to improve children's education in school with considerable success. It will repay conscientious governors handsomely to become as well-informed as they possibly can about what is happening in schools today.

In particular there have been numerous changes in the National Curriculum, so many in fact that even teachers and others working professionally in education have found it difficult to keep up with all the new folders, leaflets and circulars about topics for study, national testing arrangements or the various academic subjects. The first version of the National Curriculum in the late 1980s and early 1990s was too complex. There was little time for any pupil choice – a second foreign language, economics – or for subjects like health education. There were also far too many changes. In 1994 a committee chaired by Sir Ron Dearing tried to simplify the National Curriculum and offer a version of it that could run for several years unchanged, but even the Dearing committee exercise was not problem free. A National Curriculum must reflect the best of current knowledge and practice. It is bound to change, and governors need to keep up to date with the latest state of play.

In the following chapter we shall look at some of the issues faced in schools and frequently reported in the press and on television or radio.

Chapter 6

Issues in education

If you are lying in hospital waiting for an operation, it would be a bold patient who would instruct the surgeon where to make the incision. On the other hand we are probably entitled to know whether surgery is the only solution, when we are to be operated on, and to be listened to when describing our symptoms, apprehension or curiosity. We may be ordinary lay people, but it is our body that is being twiddled, so we are right to want to know. The relationship between lay and professional people in education is not all that different from that in the world of medicine.

Many of the major issues in education are always with us. What and how shall we teach children? Are we preparing them adequately for adult life? Sometimes, however, it is difficult for governors to join in or even understand the discussion because it may be couched in unfamiliar language. We are not referring here to the needlessly complex jargon occasionally introduced to make simple issues cloudy by inventing pretentious phrases such as 'learning stimulus materials' (toys), 'materially disadvantaged' (poor), 'endemic reduced placement opportunities' (unemployment) or 'informal decision-making sub-unit' (staffroom bridge four). It is rather that certain changes in the educational system occur suddenly, bringing with them new organisations or terminology sometimes simple in language but difficult to grasp unless one knows the background.

Thus phrases like, 'The GCSE coursework option has increased the load on the staff'; 'We need to make active tutorial work a more central part of our pastoral care system'; or 'The lower school staff are trying out diagnostic tests and profiling this year' are all simple to explain, but might not be fully understood in the first instance. In this chapter we shall take a number of issues regularly discussed by people connected with schools and sketch a little of the relevant background.

PASTORAL CARE

Looking after the welfare of children has always been a central part of the teacher's job, especially with young children, and the phrase 'pastoral care' is commonly used. In large schools, where children might easily be lost in the crowd if steps were not taken, there is often considerable planning put into looking after children's welfare. Usually the school is broken up into smaller units such as upper, middle and lower school, year groups or houses and one of the deputy heads may be given special responsibility for pastoral care.

In some schools children have a personal tutor who, if possible, stays with them through more than one year of their career. In others there may be one or more counsellors who spend much of their time advising children about their personal problems, their career or their schoolwork. Increasingly, time is scheduled specially for tutor groups to spend with the teacher assigned to look after their welfare. Some teachers draw up an elaborate programme of activities for their class so that matters of concern can be discussed. Sometimes this becomes a central part of the school's personal, social and moral development scheme.

The British tradition of counselling is different from the American style. In many American high schools there is a strong and powerful counselling department whose head has deputy principal status. Sometimes there is a conflict between the subject teachers and the counsellors about who should advise the pupil on careers or university entrance. On the other hand, where the American system works well, the pupil has a superb professional service given by trained and caring experts. In Britain there tends to be either no counsellor at all, all teachers being expected to include counselling as part of the repertoire of professional skills, or a single counsellor who works closely with teachers.

The one teacher/one class system in most primary schools allows the class teacher to take full responsibility for each child's schooling and personal welfare. The smallness of a school does not by itself, however, guarantee sound pastoral care, though it is usually there in a natural unpretentious and unsculptured way. Parents usually receive strong messages from their children that teachers either are or are not interested in their welfare.

One problem sometimes arises over records. Schools which pride themselves on good pastoral care may encourage teachers either to keep everything in their heads or to make a detailed record. If, for example, a child has been beaten by a drunken parent and a teacher discovers this, he may keep the knowledge to himself. If he leaves, however, a new teacher may not understand why the child is timid and withdrawn.

On the other hand if the first teacher, in an attempt to help his colleagues understand the child better, enters a short comment on the pupil's confidential record card, he runs the risk of being accused of biasing his colleagues against the family, or acting on gossip and hearsay. This is a difficult dilemma as one can see problems in any form of record keeping. There is some controversy over whether or not parents should be allowed to see their child's school record. It is arguable whether the children's best interests would be served by allowing this on every occasion. Some schools run two sets of records, one open for parents to see, the other confidential. In some countries there is a legal requirement that parents be permitted to see all records.

HOME AND SCHOOL

During the 1960s the importance of parents was recognised more and more and the 1970s saw a considerable increase in schools establishing parent–teacher associations or involving parents in more active participation. During the 1980s parents acquired more legal rights to choose their child's school and to receive information about their progress. Studies of children's achievement in school, both in Britain and elsewhere, show convincingly that parents' attitudes to education are crucial. Irrespective of social class, if parents strongly support their children, they do much better at school than if they show no interest.

One major stumbling block, however, is that well-meaning parents often do not know how best to help their children. We once carried out a research project at Exeter University which involved us in interviewing hundreds of parents about their children's schooling. We discovered great goodwill but massive ignorance about what was happening.

Many parents told us that they deliberately did nothing to prepare their children for school as they had been warned that they might ruin their education. We interviewed teachers to discover what it was that parents did to wreck their children's future. We got only one answer: they taught capital letters and the school taught the small letters first! Yet many of the signs that children see in their everyday life like DANGER, LOOK RIGHT or, at a zebra crossing, WAIT are written in capitals.

In the light of the interviews several schools decided to write positive letters to parents telling them how they could help prepare children for school, giving tips like 'If your child is interested in learning letters teach him the small ones first', or 'Do not push your child to learn things if he does not wish, but many children enjoy helping with shopping, listening to stories, or playing games like picture Lotto, and these are all useful and pleasant ways of preparing for school'.

Other schools put on evenings for parents to discover more about their children's schooling, not in the form of longwinded talks about new curricula, but often based on activity. One school showed parents a video of a creative writing lesson, to demonstrate how children's writing was nurtured. Another put parents into a room set out with junior school science experiments and invited them to pick up a card and do the experiment on it. Parents played with magnets and iron filings, poured liquids, discovered about sound and light, and were almost too absorbed to discuss their experiences.

At the end of a year of such experiments at involving parents in their children's education the reaction from teachers and parents was overwhelmingly favourable, and this is a common finding. Many schools which begin apprehensively, wondering if parents will come, are delighted at the response they get.

There are some problems, however. First of all, letters of invitation need to be delivered and read. Some children never give their parents the details. In multi-ethnic schools it often helps if community leaders can translate important letters into the appropriate languages, or they may be delivered but not understood. Some schools now have WELCOME signs in several languages in the school's entrance hall.

Second, the timing must be right. Some parents work shifts and cannot manage a 7.30 meeting, others have small children and need a crèche or playgroup run by volunteers if they are to come in for an evening or afternoon meeting.

Third, the occasion must be worthwhile. The secret of the success of many schools in the Exeter research was that they really involved parents. Even at upper secondary level where the subject matter is difficult, some teachers have used the assembly hall, half for the pupils to do their lesson, half for the parents to watch and eventually wander around. The annual meeting for parents, which schools have been required to hold since the 1986 Education Act, has often been badly attended. One way of ensuring a better audience is to combine the formal part of the business with the opportunity to talk individually to teachers in their classrooms.

Even schools in difficult areas can win the support of parents. One school in a town with massive social problems ran a book club. Children brought small sums of money week by week, and at monthly intervals a good children's bookseller put on a display and they cashed in their savings after school, often with their parents in attendance. This allowed high grade reading material to reach children whose homes often contained not a single book. The reading ages of the children climbed spectacularly.

Another school used parent volunteers to collect dinner money, escort children on field trips, help with games coaching and aid teachers building up a collection of magazine and newspaper cuttings. With or without a parent–teacher association there is no limit to the ingenuity of teachers who really want to involve parents. The horror stories one occasionally reads of major rows between schools and parents are often, though not always, because parents have not been fully informed of what the school is trying to do.

Some schools and local authorities have gone to much greater lengths than ever before to involve parents by putting on classes for them, so that they can better help their children at home. Various schemes have been launched, especially in the field of reading, but sometimes in mathematics as well. Parents are shown various methods of hearing their children read and are given books which they can read at home together. One example of such a scheme is PACT (Parents And Children and Teachers), which developed from a project first set up in some inner London primary schools in 1979 (see the bibliography for two books about PACT written by Alex Griffiths and Dorothy Hamilton).

Sometimes family workshops are arranged where several members of the family may come together to do craftwork, make music or pursue some other worthwhile activity. Despite all the work of the last few years there is still a great deal to be done before parents are fully in the picture, and many schools have already shown the way with good school reports, interesting evenings, easy, informal communication and teachers who take the trouble to get to know the district and community where their children live. There are now more curriculum materials available for parents and children to work together than used to be the case (see Figure 7).

MULTICULTURAL EDUCATION

In many city classrooms in Britain one finds a mixture of children from all sorts of ethnic groups, from Britain, Europe, the West Indies, Asia and Africa. The concept of multicultural education is that teachers will take into account their great variety of backgrounds. There was considerable argument about the content of a subject like history in the National Curriculum. Some people wanted more British and less European or world history. In the end the history curriculum contained all these features. Similarly there was discussion about whether religious education should deal only with Christianity, but eventually it was agreed that other world religions should be studied.

Those who advocate multicultural education are not arguing that 'if people want to live in this country they just have to fit in', nor on the other hand are they suggesting that the curriculum should be dominated by studies of Islam, the history of black Africa, soul music or the politics of South-East Asia, but rather that there should be some respect for the traditions of various ethnic groups, and that the commitment to mutual tolerance in our society is a worthy ideal.

There are many ways of working towards this objective. Schools often begin by involving parents of all communities in the life of the school, as described earlier in this chapter, and by recognising important cultural differences: that certain foods may not be eaten, that girls are not allowed out unescorted at night in some cultures, that families may wish to observe their own religious festivals.

Another possibility is to feature the customs of various groups in some public way, so that children may perform folk dances, sing songs, act plays, read poetry, or show and talk about religious ceremonies in their own region. Some teachers will offer options within their course which may be of special interest to certain pupils.

In lessons involving cookery, teachers need to be aware that some children will be vegetarians, or like eating foods cooked with certain spices. Sausage rolls may, therefore, not be something which all families will eat. In science

🐚 Parents in partnership

Places to visit

Look at the pictures.
Talk about each one and colour
the places you have visited.
Together you can write
something about your visit.

Skills: discussion; sentence writing; colouring   **Non-fiction:** *Max's book of the city of London*

4.32

Figure 7 A 'Parents in Partnership' worksheet
Source: *Flying Boot*, Ted Wragg, Thomas Nelson, 1994

lessons food tasting can involve tropical fruits like mangoes as well as the usual foods. Some teachers will go even further and attempt to tackle directly issues such as 'racial prejudice' with classes. This needs skilful handling, but if well done can contribute a great deal to harmonious race relations in a community.

The need for children to understand the lives and beliefs of others is not confined to large industrial cities with multi-ethnic communities. In schools in areas sometimes referred to as the 'white Highlands', children need to develop a broad perspective and an understanding of life in other parts of Britain and other countries where political, religious and social beliefs may be different from our own. There is no need to undertake this broader study at the expense of understanding our own culture. It would be as wrong to ignore the fact that Christianity has long been the predominant religion in Britain as it would be to pretend there is no other faith in the world; as foolish to ignore British history, geography and culture as to neglect the world perspective.

INTEGRATING CHILDREN WITH SPECIAL EDUCATIONAL NEEDS

The education of mentally and physically disabled children is an important matter which has received a great deal of publicity in recent times. Some of the debate has centred around the question of whether such children should be taught in special schools or with the rest of their group in ordinary primary and secondary schools. For some years now the word 'handicapped' has been replaced by the term 'special educational needs' (SEN).

One problem which had bedevilled special education for years is the aspiration which adults have had for SEN children. For fear of expecting too much they have sometimes expected too little. Those who believe in integration often argue that children's horizons would be raised in normal schools, whereas critics of integration feel the opposite might occur: they might become overawed by their high-achieving fellows and opt out altogether.

The Warnock Report in 1978 and the 1981 Education Act endorsed the notion that children with special educational needs should be integrated into ordinary schools where this made good sense. There are different kinds of integration, from permanent ordinary classes but with proper support facilities, to classes containing only special education pupils but with the possibility of social contacts with the other children in the school. Alongside integration, a certain number of special schools still feature prominently in the provision for children with special educational needs.

Some countries have already integrated most, if not all, SEN children into ordinary schools. It has been done for some time, for example, in Sweden, and there has been some considerable movement towards integration in many regions of the United States, so that one might find large numbers of such pupils in ordinary schools, many with cerebral palsy or more severe problems.

When integration takes place there are several implications for schools. Premises may need altering to take wheelchairs or be safer for the blind, teachers need to learn about mental and physical disability, specialist teachers need to be available who have been properly trained in the field, and close liaison with medical and social services is essential.

Furthermore the many specialist organisations for seeing, hearing and other specific disabilities need to be mobilised. People are often astonished, for example, to discover how many books have been put on cassette or produced in Braille editions, and how many aids are available from the various providers, until they encounter a blind or deaf person for the first time. Although the process of integration has been daunting and there is not universal agreement about its desirability, those many schools and colleges which have completed the process have frequently, albeit after an initially difficult period, become very committed to their policy. In schools where significant numbers of SEN children are to be found it is worth considering having on the governing body someone from the area health authority staff to facilitate communication between the health and education services.

DISRUPTIVE PUPILS

'I don't know what to do with him, but if anyone else tells me he's from a difficult home background I shall scream', said one teacher after dealing with a very anti-social 14-year-old boy. This is the dilemma a classroom teacher faces, on the one hand feeling sorry for someone who in his family life is clearly up against it, on the other hand angry at his bullying, vile language or interruption of others going peacefully about their business.

There are several kinds of disruptive pupil and many different ways of dealing with severe disruption. We are referring here not to the mild bit of cheek or inattention one finds everywhere at some time, but to the kind of pupil whose name is on every teacher's lips, and who has the ability, in full flow, to bring lessons to a complete standstill.

Disruptive behaviour is not usually caused by a single factor. For example, one might say that a pupil who does not understand what is happening in lessons will become anti-social, but there will be several others in a similar position who merely stare into space uncomprehendingly. It is usually some combination, therefore, of elements such as boredom, dislike of school in general or a teacher or pupils in particular, problems at home, and an aggressive or attention-seeking personality, which produces disruption.

Sadly, violent behaviour does appear to run in families, and parents who beat their children have often been subjected in their childhood to brutality by their own parents. A child used to the rule of the fist can be extraordinarily difficult to handle, as school sanctions are far less punitive than what he is used to, and he may simply not know yet how to respond to kindness and interest, having not encountered them before.

One remedy frequently tried is to ignore bad behaviour, but respond favourably and publicly to good behaviour, however unspectacular it may be. In some schools both in Britain and the United States there has been some success with reward systems whereby badly behaved pupils are given tokens for listening to others, waiting their turn, sitting still, getting on with their work and so on, eventually being allowed to cash in their tokens for prizes such as privileges or sweets. Perhaps obesity and dental decay are a fair swap for disruptive behaviour.

Amongst other ideas found in schools is a 'time out' or 'sin bin' system. As some disruptive pupils are hyperactive and quick to lose their self control, a cooling off period can sometimes help. The pupil leaves the classroom to go to a special unit with a teacher particularly skilful at dealing with difficult pupils. This method can work well but it needs extraordinarily sensitive handling, otherwise weak teachers opt out of their responsibilities, and the system becomes a game.

In some schools teachers become punitive, using the whole range of agreed school sanctions: withdrawal of privileges, detention or extra work. Although this too can occasionally be effective it can also result in an even more sullen and anti-social pupil, and many teachers prefer trying to win the child's confidence and respect, however wearing this may be.

Indeed some of the more notable successes have been achieved by teachers who have struggled to get through to very disturbed pupils, sometimes with the assistance of the child guidance service. There has been a significant change in the way many schools psychologists prefer to work. Whereas formerly it was accepted that problem children would be taken out of school and sent to a clinic where the psychologist would work with her wizardry, a number of specialists in child guidance, though by no means all, prefer now, wherever possible, to work with teachers in the school and tackle the problems where they occur. When this works well, teachers and psychologists find they have a much higher regard for each other, and a better understanding of what needs to be done, both to help the disruptive pupil and to protect his fellows.

If all else fails there are still some possible lines of attack. A child may be transferred to another school, which, although it often merely passes on the problem, can occasionally give a genuine fresh start. If a child is judged to be seriously maladjusted he may be sent to a specialist school for maladjusted children or to a school which has a special unit if one is available in the district.

Should the pupil be in trouble with the police the child's future may in any case be in the hands of the courts if he is to be put into care or sent away into detention. If there is a problem in the child's whole family, there is a new and now well-established tradition in some areas of whole family treatment using psychiatric social workers if necessary.

No one should underestimate, however, the wear and tear on the whole community, teachers and pupils alike, caused by the presence of one or two really disruptive pupils. There are no easy solutions, and the problems of disaffection, violence and anti-social behaviour, especially amongst adolescents of 14 or 15, remain amongst our most pressing social problems. Some teachers believe that discipline has become harder to establish and maintain in recent years, though this is hard to prove.

In extreme cases pupils may be excluded entirely from the school (Chapter 2). There was evidence in the early 1990s that pupil exclusions were on the increase. Excluding a child from school is a significant matter and is not a decision that should be taken lightly. Governors should look at the position on exclusions in their own school. If there has been a marked increase, then the question should be asked why this has happened. Governors should also look at *who* is being excluded and whether any particular groups are being excluded more frequently than others. As we pointed out in Chapter 2, parents of Afro-Caribbean boys have often complained that their children are being excluded more frequently than those from other ethnic groups.

FORMAL OR INFORMAL?

Amongst issues which regularly arouse discussion in the press is the question of teaching methods. Is traditional teaching better than progressive teaching? Are formal methods better than informal methods? The debate is not a new one.

Definitions of 'traditional' and 'progressive' or 'formal' and 'informal' are not commonly agreed, but there are some features one can describe. At its crudest a formal style implies rows of desks facing the front, the teacher addressing the whole class, all the children engaged on the same task, no freedom of movement without the teacher's permission, stress on completion and academic achievement, and regular testing.

An equally rough and ready caricature of informal teaching suggests tables placed around the room in no particular order, children working individually or in small groups, the teacher walking around monitoring what they are doing, freedom for children to go the resources area, to paint, do maths, pursue their project, or to read as they decide, stress on co-operation and social development, and individual records of each child's progress.

One reason why the discussion sometimes causes wrath is that we all like to believe we were fairly well educated, or at least that what happened to us in school did us no harm, and that anything different might be an experiment on children, a raw deal for society, or even a needless risk. As ever, the argument often centres around stereotypes which barely exist. Most teachers use a mixture of styles, addressing the whole class when appropriate, sometimes working in groups, allowing freedom of movement in certain phases of the lesson but not others, and determining what children do on some occasions whilst allowing choice on others.

Fears that the education system is saturated with way-out informal teachers whose classes never do any decent work are exaggerated. Teachers can often succeed using any style of teaching to which they are strongly committed. What is critical is not so much the style, but the skill with which it is applied. Informal teaching is very difficult to do well and demands a great deal of the teacher, who needs good class management, great mobility, proper record keeping and considerable inventiveness.

We once did a case study of the informal teacher whose children obtained highest gains in a research study. She had excellent relationships with her class, and ensured that everyone worked hard by getting around to every pupil and sometimes publicly taking stock. She would, for example, review progress by saying suddenly, 'Now you two are doing your maths, and John and Peter you're still working on assembly. Mary, I think it's probably about time you were leaving that.' It was a light touch but everyone knew that she had complete grasp of each child's progress. The work-rate of her pupils was the highest we ever recorded in either a formal or an informal classroom.

It is true, unfortunately, that the lessons of teachers who attempt informal teaching and are not able to handle it with skill can be very unproductive. Children 'slow-time' the teacher by spinning out a half-hour task into a half or whole day, and learn very little else, other than to dislike the school. Equally, however, an unskilled formal teacher can bore children to distraction by talking most of the time and allowing little or no individual work. Most of us have, at some time, been bored and learned little, simply because the teacher 'socked it to us', with few opportunities to do something for ourselves.

At the heart of skilful informal teaching often lies sensitive handling of project work. A project is undertaken either by the whole class or on an individual or small group basis. Thus a primary school class may spend a few weeks doing a project on 'Our village', but individuals may opt for something of personal interest like 'horses', 'railways' or 'farming' (see Figure 8).

By devoting a considerable amount of time to projects which have captured their imagination children will read and write a great deal, and will have to learn how to find and use information, as well as how to organise their time. A teacher's scheme for a class project on 'Our village' (p. 136) shows how wide-ranging the topic can be when properly planned and thought out.

The formal versus the informal debate will continue, but no one yet has proved conclusively that a way of operating by itself is critical. Nevertheless, questions about teaching methods must always be asked by both professionals and the lay public. Such questioning is entirely healthy provided that sensibly worked out new teaching methods, thought to be more effective, or more suitable to changed conditions or improvements in our knowledge, are permitted. Schools where nothing changes are as undesirable as those where

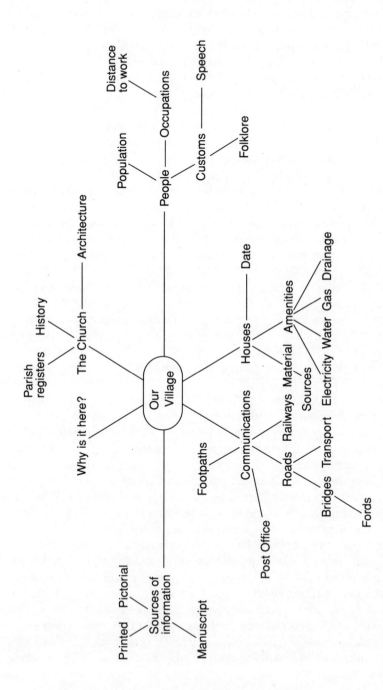

Figure 8 A project diagram showing how the topic 'Our Village' might be studied
Source: Changing the Primary School, John Blackie, Macmillan, 1974

nothing is ever the same, and new methods can only prove themselves if given a decent chance to run and if subjected to regular and deliberate evaluation.

GROUPING FOR TEACHING AND LEARNING

'Setting', 'streaming', 'banding', 'mixed ability teaching' are all terms used to describe how children are grouped in schools. Most primary schools use classes of mixed ability, and in recent years this pattern has spread to a number of secondary schools. It is perhaps most helpful to give a short description of the meaning of each of these terms, in so far as there is any agreement about them, and to mention some advantages and disadvantages commonly attributed to each.

Streaming

Streaming was for many schools the traditional way of grouping pupils. Some indication of *general* ability was sought; it might be the result of an intelligence test or, more likely, it would be the child's performance in end of year exams. Thus the brightest children were put into the A stream, the next brightest into the B stream, and so on, right down to the D or E stream, or even the fourteenth or fifteenth stream in a few very large secondary schools. The advantage seemed to be that the teacher, having a thin band of ability range in his class, could keep children occupied at the appropriate level, stretching the brightest and moving slowly with lower streams.

Critics argued that the system was insensitive, as some pupils are good at maths, poor at French and vice versa, and led to the 'self-fulfilling prophecy', whereby children in the D stream, feeling they are the 'sink' or the 'thickies', become anti-social and unambitious. A further problem was the low transfer rate between streams, which meant people placed in a low or high stream were probably destined to stay there.

Setting

Setting was partly designed to combat criticism of the insensitivity of streaming by general ability and is a form of streaming by *specific* ability. A child may be in set 3 for English, set 1 for maths, set 2 for French, set 5 for science, and so on. Objectors argue that some children are put in high sets for everything and others in low sets for all their lessons, so the 'sink' mentality and the self-fulfilling prophecy still apply, the bright get better and the dull are given lower horizons and still become anti-school.

Mixed ability

Mixed ability was an attempt to give everyone a fair chance by having classes containing the whole ability range found in the school. Thus on intake children will be put randomly into classes all containing a mixture of backgrounds and abilities. It was hoped that this would remove the difficult D stream problem, and avoid the premature labelling of children as bright or dull at an age when poor self-esteem might crucially affect learning.

Critics of mixed ability grouping argue that the assignment is too difficult for most teachers, that bright children become bored, and the less able are left behind as the teacher struggles to cater for the average pupil. They also point to the massive amount of preparatory and recording work necessary if the teacher is to do mixed ability teaching sensitively, ensuring each child is engaged in something appropriate to his ability and interests. Most primary school classes are now of mixed ability and there is continuing argument about how far it should spread into secondary schools.

Banding

Banding is for many schools a compromise between streaming and mixed ability teaching. Sympathising with some of the aspirations of mixed ability enthusiasts, but not wishing to span the whole ability range, they operate usually via two or three broad bands of ability. For example a school with an entry of eight classes of children each year may have three bands, band 1 containing three classes of brighter children, band 2 with three classes of average ability, and band 3 having two classes of slower learners. Within each band the classes are of equal ability and take parallel courses. The argument advanced against banding is that it still labels children as A, B or C.

Other possibilities

People can be grouped for learning in any way one chooses. For many years children were grouped by *sex*, with boys and girls educated separately. We take it for granted that children of the *same age* should be educated together irrespective of their ability yet in some primary schools 'vertical' or 'family' grouping is practised, whereby 5- to 7-year-olds are put together, and there has been a remarkable breed of practitioner, in one- and two-teacher rural schools, who has coped with 5- to 11- or even 5- to 15-year-olds in the same class. In smaller sixth forms 16- to 19-year-olds may be in the same group, and adult education caters for evening classes containing adolescents, the middle-aged and retired people, from 13 or 14 up to 70 or 80.

Teachers of mathematics and French often opted out of the mixed ability pattern (though a few did not, with conspicuous success) on the grounds that these are linear subjects. In order to learn B you must have learned A first, it was said; and certainly it is the case that in most secondary schools which do have mixed ability classes for the first two or three years, the mathematicians and linguists are likely to prefer setting from the beginning or after the first year.

" EARLY SPECIALISATION "

Some people have even argued that the National Curriculum levels of attainment should be the basis of grouping. This would mean that all the children, say, at Level 4, which is the point that the average 11-year-old should have reached, would be in the same group. The problem here is that a slow 13-year-old, average 11-year-old and a bright 8-year-old could all be in the same class.

Successful teachers of mixed ability classes use a judicious mixture of whole class teaching, individual and small group work, and spend many hours creating workbooks, workcards, and resource material. Almost invariably they keep detailed records of children's work. There can be no hard and fast rule about grouping children for learning. What suits one school is simply not appropriate for another. A key factor, however, is the commitment of those who have to work the system.

SPECIALISATION

At Key Stage 3 of the National Curriculum, 11- to 14-year-olds have to follow the whole set of ten subjects. At Key Stage 4, however, there is more space for options when children are in the 14 to 16 age group. By comparison with many other countries the British educational system has always been condensed, and this was often due in part to early specialisation which narrowed choices for pupils at 13 or 14 by asking them to choose between, say, more science, another language and practical subjects. Thus relatively young secondary pupils would be making a critical decision which might already be determining whether they would eventually join the arts or science sixth form.

At the 16+ stage in England and Wales pupils will probably specialise in two, three or four subjects (whereas their counterparts in many European countries or in the USA would still be studying in several fields), and at 18 they may go on to complete a three-year degree programme. Meanwhile similar students elsewhere might at 19 embark on a four-year degree course, or, in Germany for example, on an open-ended university career which might last for at least six or seven years. This early specialisation in Britain produces graduates at 21 as compared with 23-, 24- or 25-year-old graduates abroad.

Critics of early specialisation have tried to secure a broader curriculum through revision of the examination system. Various sixth form examination patterns have been proposed over the years, some necessitating an arts/science mix, others requiring the sixth former to take exams at two levels, as in the Schools Council proposals made in the late 1970s which proposed three subjects at Normal (N) and two at Further (F) level. Some educationists favour the pattern of the International Baccalaureate, which not only requires pupils to study a wider range of subjects, but has an added recommendation of being widely accepted abroad in an age when international recognition of qualifications obtained in various countries is becoming increasingly important.

In 1988 the Higginson Committee recommended that sixth formers should take five equally weighted subjects, but at that time the government said it preferred a mixture of traditional A levels and the Advanced Supplementary (A/S) level examination.

The National Curriculum, by requiring all pupils to take a science or language up to the age of 16, has reduced some aspects of early specialisation. Nevertheless, unexciting science teaching and outstanding English teaching in a school may produce a dearth of science and a glut of English specialists. Similarly, strong sex stereotyping, whereby it is subtly suggested that girls ought not to do science, for example, can bring about the situation which has occurred in Britain, producing three or four times as many boys taking A-level physics as girls. Yet in other countries girls may take science on the same scale as boys and go on in sizeable numbers to become engineers, technicians or physicists.

The Equal Opportunities Act, which made it illegal for someone to be denied the opportunity to take a subject on offer in the school on the grounds of sex alone, as well as some changes in attitude generally, have led to more girls specialising in science and technology in recent times. However, the numbers of pupils taking high level examinations in vital subjects like maths, physics and chemistry fell during the 1980s and 1990s. One feature of the entry to higher education during that same period has been the increasing percentage of girls going on to universities. If more girls chose to specialise in these important subjects, then national shortages would not be a problem.

TESTS AND EXAMINATIONS

The concern for accountability in education often tends to focus on examinations and testing. Tests, it is argued, will show whether or not schools are delivering the goods, and there is some support for this idea. Dissenters, on the other hand, point to the evils of the 'payment by results' system in use before the turn of the century, when schools for poorer children in city centres were starved of resources and this served to compound rather than alleviate children's misfortune. One of the concerns, mentioned above, about the proposals in the 1988 Education Act for tests at 7, 11, 14 and 16 was that, badly handled, they might lead to a two- or three-tier system with parents flocking to the upmarket, high scoring schools.

In the 1960s and 1970s there was a massive shift in the public examining pattern. The 11+ examination, designed to help local authorities assign pupils to secondary schools, declined sharply as comprehensive reorganisation spread, but the 16+ increased considerably over the same period.

Whereas formerly about 20 to 25 per cent of the age group would take a public examination like the GCE, once CSE had been set up, ostensibly for children in the middle band of ability, the position changed rapidly. By the late 1980s about 90 per cent of pupils were leaving school having taken O-level or CSE examinations. The fusion of GCE and CSE, the General Certificate of Secondary Education (GCSE), produced its first cohort in 1988. It was a radically different examination which stressed enquiry and investigation in fields like mathematics or science, and skill at communication in modern languages. Marks obtained for coursework could contribute to the final grade, and this was typically a fifth or a quarter but could even be higher. The pressure on pupils and teachers is quite considerable in such an examination.

The examination for 17-year-olds, the Certificate in Prevocational Education (CPVE), was another radical kind of assessment based on profiles rather than on three-hour examinations. The Advanced Supplementary (A/S) level, equivalent to half an A level, is another product of the 1980s proliferation of public examinations. In the 1990s there were attempts to develop National Vocational Qualifications that could have equal standing to traditional GCSE or A levels.

Clearly, too strong an emphasis on testing would produce a very narrow curriculum with teachers under pressure to coach for the test. On the other hand a sensible programme of testing can provide useful measures of the extent to which knowledge and skills are being acquired, attitudes are changing, or objectives are being realised.

There have been several new technical developments in testing in the last few years. Whereas in the past many examinations consisted exclusively of essay questions, amongst techniques currently used are:

- *Oral tests.* Interviews with pupils, tape-recording of conversations in a foreign language, etc.
- *Multiple choice tests.* The pupil has to circle the correct answer from a set of possibilities, only one of which is correct, the others acting as distracters, e.g. *Britain declared war on Germany in 1939 because:*

A   The Archduke of Austria was assassinated by a German.

B   Germany and Austria signed a treaty.

C   U-boats had been sinking British passenger ships.

D   Hitler occupied Poland and refused to withdraw.

E   German planes bombed London.

- *Graded tests.* Like the driving test these are pass/fail tests, sometimes called 'criterion-referenced' tests. Instead of gaining a mark out of 100 the pupil simply passes or fails and may take the examination again until successful. Certain examinations have always been organised like this and the idea is spreading. In French, for example, Level 1 might be an indication of the pupil's understanding of simple French, Level 2 the pupil's ability to sustain simple conversation on everyday topics, Level 3 being able to translate for a friend, and so on.

In 1988 the Task Group on Assessment and Testing (TGAT) produced a report proposing that the national tests at 7, 11, 14 and 16 required by the 1988 Education Act should use a ten-point scale. Seven-year-old pupils would probably score at Levels 1, 2 and 3; children aged 11 at roughly Level 3, 4 and 5, perhaps even 6; children aged 14 might achieve at Levels 4, 5, 6 and 7. In its early stages this programme was bedevilled by testing boycotts, as teachers protested at the workload or at the very nature of the tests themselves. Since 1995 the ten level have been reduced to eight, with the former Levels 9 and 10 renamed 'Exceptional performance'.

CHANGING PUPIL NUMBERS

Until the late 1970s most people thought that falling rolls were what you got when the baker's delivery boy dropped his basket. They were much more devastating. From 1954 to 1964 the birth figures climbed steadily, reaching around 900,000 in 1964. Each year after that they dropped steadily and then sharply, falling below 600,000 in the late 1970s and producing the lowest birth cohorts since the 1930s when some people thought that the British people would be extinct by the year 2000. From 1977 they rose again.

The consequences are clear to see. When the birth figures drop by over one-third in quite a short time the effects are bound to ripple right through the education system. First of all primary school rolls fell in the 1970s as the leaner years began to enter full-time schooling. Secondary school rolls reached peak size in 1978 and 1979 but numbers then fell until the mid-1990s. Higher education was not really affected, as more and more pupils stayed on in education voluntarily. Teacher training was decimated as fewer teachers were required, and many colleges of education were forced to close or merge.

In primary schools the effects of *falling* pupil numbers are considerable but manageable, as the 'one teacher one class' system allows natural wastage when someone leaves or retires. In secondary schools, where most teachers are subject specialists, the effects are worse. Promotion is harder to come by, the school may no longer be able to offer all it could when it was larger, and early retirement and redundancies have to be faced.

Falling rolls have different effects on different schools. If there is a drop in the national birthrate of a third, then not all schools suffer to the same extent. A secondary school of 900 pupils, in an inner-city area where the population is moving away or being rehoused, may fall to 300 pupils or be closed down. In a more typical area it will drop to 600 pupils. On the other hand, if sited in a new town, near an expanding housing estate or a popular suburb, it may stay at 900 or increase to over 1000.

Rising enrolments began to affect primary schools from 1985, and secondary schools from the early 1990s. Rising rolls usually bring a need for temporary classrooms, more teachers and resources, and more new schools. Governors will, therefore, hear about rising numbers in both the primary and the secondary sector, and this may be their most pressing organisational problem.

Again it should be noted that not all schools are equally affected, and even if the national birthrate is going up, school populations in some areas may actually go down. Those governors who are not too old might consider breeding for Britain, on the grounds that each new child will provide employment for a twentieth of a teacher or so, and help look after the rest of us in our old age when all the low birthrate years have to work like two people to pay for our vitamin pills and false teeth.

A SCHOOL ON THE RUN

All the issues depicted above pale into insignificance when a school becomes the victim of adverse publicity and finds itself on the run. The effect on staff, pupils, parents and the whole community can be considerable and the mass media play an important role.

The relationship between the educational system and the media is a curious one. For some reason bad news about schools is good news for newspapers, so that teachers are often dismayed when the local press, having ignored all their exam results, the pupils who painted old people's bungalows, or collected a million lollipop sticks for Oxfam, devote half a page to the school's one glue sniffer.

William Taylor, writing about the press's negative reaction in the first years of the secondary modern school, cited many extracts from newspaper cuttings in the early days which gleefully emphasised vandalism, low standards or scandal. Comprehensive schools have suffered in the same way, as have informal teaching methods and new curricula.

One of the present writers was concerned with an independent enquiry into a school set up in response to huge press coverage of complaints by a small group of parents. Newspapers had devoted pages to the accusations,

TV and radio had covered the setting up of the enquiry and national politicians who had never been within 100 miles of the school were calling for dismissals and resignations. When the report of the independent group was published stating that there was no substance to the accusations and that the overwhelming majority of parents supported the school, no national paper showed any interest and TV and radio were silent. Only the local newspapers carried brief reports.

Consequently it is vital for all schools to have good relations and effective communication between staff, parents, local and regional media and governors. It is quite common for governors, head, teachers or parents to be interviewed when some problem has occurred, and if public strife is fuelled it is hard for the school to recover and for scars to be healed.

When angry people write to MPs or the Secretary of State, demand enquiries, say in the press or on TV that they are 'appalled' or 'disgusted', something has gone seriously awry. It could happen to any school one day no matter how carefully it goes about its business, and in tightly-knit communities the people concerned may never recover.

It is therefore crucial for governors to take advice from their fellows, from teachers and the head and from people knowledgeable about schools in general or about the events concerned in particular before expressing opinions publicly which may be based on inaccurate or erroneous information. There is nothing worse than governors giving an instant opinion to the press, and then regretting it later when it turns out they were wrongly informed. The skilful use of local newspapers, radio and television is most important. If there has been plenty of good news, then a school can more easily weather a single piece of bad luck.

SCHOOL INSPECTION

'We're going to be inspected.' As soon as that statement is uttered in a primary or a secondary school mass panic follows. Even well run schools with nothing to hide or fear can feel a strong sense of apprehension at the thought of a group of external heavies trampling though the premises, sniffing in the cupboards, looking for skeletons.

There are several forms of inspection. A local authority can send in its own inspectors, not only if a school is doing badly, but on a routine basis. With the many staffing cuts in LEAs since money was devolved to schools in the early 1990s, such inspections have become less common. Similarly, if the school is offering certain examination courses, including vocational courses, there may be visits from external examiners, to look at facilities, give oral or practical tests to pupils, check the staff's marking and assessment procedures. Premises may also be inspected on safety, health, or different grounds, by the fire service or other authority.

The most apprehension, however, occurs when the Office for Standards in

Education (OFSTED) arrives. Back in the old days many teachers served their whole career and found their teaching was inspected only once, or not at all, by a member of Her Majesty's Inspectorate (HMI). Since 1992 OFSTED has tried to inspect all schools on a regular basis. Instead of HMI doing them, these inspections are carried out by teams of inspectors who operate as a private company, putting in a tender for each inspection contract. The team varies in size, according to the number of pupils on roll, but it consists of a registered inspector, who acts as team leader, a lay inspector, who does not work professionally in education, and other specialists, depending on age group or subjects.

The school is usually asked for a great deal of preliminary information. The inspection will last for several days, and the school is supposed to function 'normally' (but try telling that to the teachers who have stayed up half the night preparing their lessons!). The inspections are very thorough, and attempts are made to find out the views of parents and members of the community, not just to look at exam results, resources and classroom teaching. All the details of how the inspection is to be carried out, what information is required, and what happens afterwards, are described in official publications which governors should be able to see.

Following the inspection there is a written report to the governors which is also available to the press and public. It must be discussed at a governors' meeting, and the recommendations in it must be heeded. If a school gets an unsatisfactory report then it will be called to account later, when it must demonstrate what it has done to improve and implement recommendations. If it is still deemed to be failing, then stern action will follow and control of the school may pass away from the local authority.

In principle the idea of regular inspection every few years is fine. Unfortunately, the language of inspections reports is often dominated by 'performance indicators' and bureaucratic matters. There is often great stress on the school being 'above', 'at or near', or 'below' the national average on such matters as test scores or truancy. The reports are often littered with phrases like 'generally satisfactory', and prominence is often given to the school's development plan, or the legality or otherwise of its morning assembly.

These are all important matters, but teachers and governors often feel depressed that what they regard as a matter of central importance has not figured as centrally as they would like. In tough inner city schools people have often felt upset at the significance attached to the school's examination scores being below the national average, when all concerned are trying to work in difficult circumstances.

OFSTED inspections will change in form as experience is gained, but whatever form they take it is up to governors to make the best of what may well be an insightful report into matters of concern, even if there is cause for dissent and a few bruised feelings. Many teachers nowadays feel scrutinised to death by press and public. Sensitive governors will recognise the emotions involved and understand the anxiety, while helping create a positive climate for progress. In a really good school people will see an OFSTED report as part of a continuous appraisal of what the school does, something to take on board as part of a constant quest to improve, not as a set of commandments or an administrative paper chase.

NEW TECHNOLOGY

First it was radio, then films, records, television, teaching machines, slides, tapes and so on. Today's 'new technology' is tomorrow's 'old technology'. Now we have microcomputers, word processors, CD ROMs, Virtual Reality, the Information 'Superhighway', and a host of others. Governors often wonder which are the toys and gimmicks and which the genuine benefits to education. It is an inescapable feature of our modern world that learning and information technology play an important part in it. Most of our bills and records of transactions are now computerised. Children have to learn to use new technology and also learn from it. It does not replace the pen or the book, but it enhances it. Schools buy what they can afford and what aids learning and teaching.

The major feature of the newer educational technology is the *interactive* nature of it. Such is the memory power of modern machinery that vast stores of knowledge can be stored in tiny spaces and then cross-questioned. A few years ago copper wires held just twelve telephone calls. Today the fibre optic, a thin strand of glass like a human hair, can carry a billion calls. A huge mainframe computer costing millions of pounds is only about four times as powerful as a table-top games machine costing hundreds of pounds. Make sure you try out for yourself your school's newest machines. Why should the children have all the fun?

Chapter 7

Difficult situations

In this section we have included some tricky cases that can come your way as a governor, and we suggest some ways in which you might react. We do not propose, however, that our solutions are necessarily the best. On some occasions being right, and asserting that you are right, is not the best way to solve a problem.

It would be a useful exercise for you first to read the 'problem' and to use your commonsense on it. Then compare our comments with your own judgement. Sometimes our comments are brief, but where the problems are complex our comments are fuller. These problems, incidentally, are all based on actual events that have come to governors' meetings for discussion.

BEING SUED

Problem

Shortly after the beginning of the A-level examinations an angry complaint is received that one of your pupils had been given a wrong set book to study by her teacher. This error came to light only after the pupil had first opened the question paper in the examination hall. She was most distraught and the parents threatened legal action against the school.

Comment

Unfortunately things like these do happen from time to time. The A-level Examination Boards are well aware of it and are usually prepared to make allowances for it in working out the scores of affected candidates. The head should have notified the Board immediately.

It is not so easy however to work out what effect the *shock* might have had on the pupil's performance. At one time parents and pupils would have had to put all this down to experience. Certainly they could complain to the LEA which might issue a reprimand or even take disciplinary action against the teacher concerned. Beyond that there seems to be little that could be done.

As the result of a court case in 1994 it seems however that the way may be now more open than previously for parents to sue schools or local education authorities for such negligence. After all, if a surgeon performs an incorrect operation or the newly built extension to our house falls down, we are entitled to sue for compensation. Commonsense suggests that something similar should apply to schools.

It is not easy for parents or adult pupils to sue. They must convince the courts that proper and reasonable care has not been taken (*perfection* in these matters is not necessary). They must also show what loss or injury they have incurred because of the error, since without this the courts cannot calculate adequate compensation. Nevertheless this is an opening which parents will surely exploit with the passing of time. Governors would be wise to check their insurance cover for such matters carefully.

ALLEGATIONS OF CHILD ABUSE

Problem

A pupil in your school has complained to your deputy head teacher that a teacher has sexually abused him or her. Details of time and place are given and the allegation, though surprising, looks plausible. The head has immediately sent the teacher home on suspension, and has reported the matter to the governors and the LEA.

Comment

Parents and governors rightly are revolted by such activities and passions run high. The head has done the right thing. School governors should however tread very warily indeed. The whole issue of child abuse figured prominently in the media during the early 1990s in the wake of some horrific events. Society expressed its concern, for example, through the Children Act which gave welfare services greater powers and duties. Sympathy for children increased in intensity: a well-known media presenter told millions of viewers dramatically: 'Children do not lie.'

There is no doubt about what must happen if the allegations are true. The full power of the law must be invoked and the teacher concerned dismissed, sent to jail, or whatever the law deems appropriate in the circumstances. The main problem for governors in these *proven* cases is the aftermath, the devastating effect not only on the child but on other children in the school, the feeling of sleaze which affects all, even the innocent, the anxiety of parents, the recriminations – how could it happen? There are invariably repercussions for all teachers, even those beyond reproach. Some reports suggest that single teachers are less welcome in schools, particularly boarding schools, than was once the case.

A big problem for governors is the *unproven* or, even worse, the *unfounded* allegation. On occasion, some children *do* fabricate a story – sometimes recklessly without thought for the consequences, on occasion, perhaps, to achieve notoriety, and sometimes, it must be said, maliciously.

Governors need to keep at the front of their mind what happens to the teacher who is the target of such an allegation. The teacher is immediately sent home under a cloud. The Child Protection Unit of the LEA investigates, as will the police. Other children who may have been witnesses or who might have a contribution to make are interviewed at length. For some younger children it all seems like an exciting episode of a TV crime series. By now what has been *alleged* has spread through the school community like wildfire, with exaggeration and invention. Anxious parents come to school, some demanding to know whether the teacher will be allowed to return. The local press reports 'Horror at Primrose School – Parents Demand Action!'

Such cases can drag on for months. There have, sadly, been cases where, after it is all over, teachers *against whom nothing whatsoever has been proven* have been refused their jobs back because relationships with parents have broken down irrevocably. In another case it was eventually shown that the pupil who had made serious and detailed accusations against a senior member of staff was actually away from school on the day the alleged offence took place in school, and too young to be prosecuted for wasting police time and causing such protracted distress. Sadly, mud sticks. Would *you* appoint to your school a teacher about whom there were nasty rumours? Unsubstantiated allegations have ruined blameless careers and caused breakdowns in teachers' own family relationships.

Sympathy for children is not grounds for denying basic legal rights to teachers, who are particularly vulnerable. In such situations governors need to bear in mind that *everyone* is presumed innocent until *proven* guilty, and that, as employers, they have an obligation to follow the law and good practice on behalf of all concerned.

RUNNING OUT OF MONEY

Problem

Your school has had a difficult spring term because more staff than usual have been absent with 'flu. Your budget for staff wages and salaries has been badly overspent in employing supply teachers to keep the teaching going. It looks as if you are going to finish the financial year with a deficit.

Comment

This is only one of many unforeseen items of expenditure which can hit schools. You should have set up an 'emergency' or 'contingency' fund within your budget, so there may be cash there which you can raid. Otherwise you will have to look at what is left in all your other budgets and claw back from them what you need to correct the overspend.

It may be a good idea to have meetings, say once a term, to move money around between budget headings as the need arises. It may also make sense to put money *into* budgets once a term rather than once a year: this reduces the problems which can arise because budget holders, craftily guessing that you will at some stage try to get some of *their* money back, have spent their money for the whole year very quickly.

Schools may also insure themselves against costs arising from staff absences. Your LEA may have a scheme. Be careful, though, to read the small print. A policy which comes to life only when your school has been shut for a week is no use. And if your school has a bad time during the 'flu term, so also will others: next year the premiums will go up astronomically. The extent to which other teachers *must* help out when colleagues are absent is now closely regulated by their 'Baker contracts' which we have described in Chapter 2. If you try to reduce your budget deficit that way, remember that you are trading on goodwill only.

It sometimes worries governors that they may be held personally responsible if they fail to manage their budget properly. Independent schools which are charities are required to submit their accounts to the Charity Commission for oversight, and grant-maintained schools to the DFE. LEA schools with delegated budgets are responsible to their LEA. Only in very rare and extreme cases where governors can be shown to have been grossly negligent or have failed to see what was staring them in the face can governors be held personally liable. LEAs, incidentally, have power to take a school budget back from governors and run it themselves. Spending school funds on a governors' outing to the seaside and a pub is definitely actionable.

When faced with cash shortages or with having to sack teachers, some governing bodies have threatened 'to set illegal budgets'. However much we may sympathise with fellow governors in times of financial hardship, we question whether they should act in this way (although the threat might just produce more money!!).

These governors appear to concede that what they propose is unlawful. That implies that they are deliberately failing to manage their budgets in the way the law requires, which can result only in the LEA taking the budget back from them, as we noted above. Presumably then the cuts which the governors sought to avoid would be implemented anyway. The issue is really: who is more likely to do what has to be done with the best interests of your school at heart, you or the LEA?

Whereas governors are protected against accidental overspending or overspending in good faith, it is very doubtful whether intentional overspending of this sort is acceptable within the law. Who, for example, would have to pay staff salaries when the budget was empty halfway through the year? Since you created the problem, you as governors and individuals would probably have to! That could be very unpleasant.

Governors of maintained and grant maintained schools who might think of taking this step should perhaps compare their position with that of the governors of fee-paying schools. The latter can charge in fees only what parents are prepared to pay – otherwise their schools close. If they set a budget to spend more than they have, there is no guarantee that parents will come to their aid and pay more in fees. It is more than likely that the school will have to close.

BREAKING THE LAW ON MORNING WORSHIP

Problem

Your head teacher reports that she is having great difficulty in ensuring that regular morning worship takes place as the law requires. She is agnostic and does not take part herself, but accepts fully that it is part of her job to see that it takes place. Many of her staff are exercising their right not to help. A complaint has been received from a Muslim parent that the assemblies are all Christian in tone.

Comment

Morning assembly has been a traditional part of life in UK schools. It must by law be undenominational Christian in character. Denominational schools of course will hold assemblies according to their faith. In LEA and grant maintained schools parents may withdraw their children from worship – the children must however be in school and are not allowed simply to turn up late. The same applies to teaching staff.

You may have to pay for outside help if you cannot keep the system going. It may help to know that it is not a requirement that the whole school meet at the same time in the same place: many schools simply do not have any one room large enough to contain a full assembly. Some staff *may* be willing to take more than one assembly.

It is sufficient if most assemblies in any one term are generally Christian, and this may pacify the Muslim parent. It must be said, however, that the law is a nonsense in those schools where members of faiths other than Christian are in the majority, sometimes vast majority. One can only wonder at a system whereby a tiny handful of Christians pupils attend morning worship. This is not the spirit of collective worship intended when the Act was drawn up in 1944. Society has changed greatly since then. In 1994 the Office for Standards in Education (OFSTED) described daily acts of worship in secondary schools as 'disappointing', but a government circular reinforced the Christian aspects and stressed the importance of teaching about Jesus.

It may well be the case that yours is a school which breaks the law very quietly for practical reasons which seem to you to be strong. Some take a very elastic view of what the term 'Christian' means. However, if a parent were to complain to the DFE or your LEA you might well receive a letter in an asbestos envelope ordering you to mend your ways, and it is certainly something that will be looked at during an OFSTED inspection. The Secretary of State may decide to *order* – a very serious step – the governors of a school to carry out the exact requirements of the law. The Minister is entitled to ask the courts for backup: if a school refuses, the consequences could be very nasty. However it is most unlikely that the courts would ever require the impossible: they may insist that you try harder, though.

COMPLAINTS ABOUT DISCIPLINE

Problem

Mrs Jones has written to the chair about a teacher who, it is alleged, is not handling her daughter properly. She is a good girl at home, but is not used to being told to do things. Mrs Jones believes that children should learn discipline from within and not being pushed about.

Comment

As governors you should first refer this to the head teacher, who is appointed by you to look after the internal management of the school. Only when this has been done should you write back to the parent. Your role is only to satisfy yourselves that this is not the tip of some unpleasant iceberg. Teachers' jobs would be quite impossible if each of their twenty-five or so charges had to be treated exactly according to parents' wishes. Would the principle apply to children of bad parents as well as of good? And who would decide whether each parent was good or bad?

The law gives teachers the status of *parents*. They use their training to look after a much bigger family, the classes they teach. They have to consider the well-being of *all* the members of their families, which means that they must bring to bear their skills of organisation, management and discipline. Because teachers are like *third parents* to the children, no other parent can dictate precisely how each child is to be treated. The law assumes teachers will use a style of control that suits the majority of 'reasonable' parents.

WHO CARES ABOUT SMOKING?

Problem

A pupil at your school has been punished for smoking on her way to school. The parents are livid and say that you have no right to do this because it is an infringement of their 15-year-old's personal liberty – and it happened outside school anyway. They intend to keep their daughter away from school until they receive an apology.

Comment

We mentioned earlier that it is the job of every school to look after the general interests of *all* its pupils to the best of its judgement. Sometimes teachers and parents will disagree, just as mothers and fathers sometimes do. Neither is always right, neither always wrong. Reasonable school rules are part of the law of the land. A concern for children's health is obviously part of any school's job, and to work this into school rules as part of a general health education policy is commonplace.

If a youngster goes to a party on a Saturday night and misbehaves in some way, few parents would take the view that because the misbehaviour was not at home it was none of their business. Teachers are in the same position. They, like parents, have a right to expect that their pupils will follow school rules away from school.

However – and it is an important qualification – this could easily lead to a situation where parents and schools were permanently at loggerheads. What would have happened, for example, if a teacher from your school by chance had seen the same pupil smoking with her parents while both were on holiday in France?

The law has then had to establish a line of demarcation where the authority of the school finishes and that of the parents begins. Thus anything a day school pupil does on the journey to and from school is very much the concern of the school and parents cannot wilfully obstruct it. Boarding schools of course have 24-hours-per-day authority over their pupils during term time, even when out of school.

AT LAST. THEY'VE GONE. NO, THEY HAVEN'T

Problem

Wayne and Shane have caused mayhem in your school for at least eighteen months. They have almost driven a member of staff to resign and the head teacher is at her wits' end to know how best to deal with the problem. Finally, after a particularly nasty incident the head permanently excludes the boys and as governors you give full approval.

The parents appeal to the governors, as is their right. As chair of the appeals panel which the governors set up, the head teacher confirms the decision to exclude the boys. She tells the parents that they have wasted the governors' time, as the case against their boys is unanswerable. The parents storm out saying that they are going to a solicitor.

Comment

You have made a mess of this one and the parents are likely to win. No doubt Wayne and Shane will wreak vengeance in their customary way. The error was to include the head teacher in the appeal panel, and even worse that the head was appointed as chair.

" THERE IS COMPLETE AGREEMENT BETWEEN MYSELF AND THE CHAIRMAN OF GOVERNORS"

When we make any formal appeal we expect it to be heard by independent people who have not previously been involved with the case. The idea is that they should come with uncluttered minds. This clearly was not the case here. It was the head who brought the charges against the boys in the first place –

she obviously had an axe to grind at the appeal. Any court would, to use the technical term, 'strike down' the decision of the appeal panel. The boys would return to school until a new appeal could be heard. If you mess this one up you could be said to be harassing the boys.

You may now have another legal problem. If all the governors are fully and painfully acquainted with the problem, where are you going to find truly independent members of a second appeal panel? You should really have seen to it that some governors were kept in reserve.

Formal appeals to governors against expulsion from independent schools are rare and there is usually no mechanism for having them heard. Judges have commented unfavourably on this. The reason is that parents who send their children to independent schools are entering into a private and personal agreement to accept the school reasonably as it is. They are not obliged, after all, to enter into the agreement in the first place.

Nevertheless it is an odd discrepancy that one is entitled to an appeal over say a minor parking fine, but not about a major event in any pupil's life, expulsion from school. There is also the possibility of whether vindictiveness is going unchecked behind the scenes. As Winston Churchill wrote, 'The powers of the headmasters of the great public schools of this country are such as even Prime Ministers may envy.'

The fact that the head teacher was chosen to chair the appeal panel should alert us to another matter which can be troublesome for governors. The head (unless she has chosen not to be) is a fellow governor: she is respected on the governing body and personal relationships are both friendly and good. Many governors see disagreements with the head teacher almost as akin to letting a friend down. But in many matters – exclusion is only one – the function of the governing body is to review what has taken place and to correct it where necessary.

Depriving pupils of their education at your school, particularly if it is to be permanent, is a very serious step to take. It is a human rights issue: the European Convention on Human Rights which the UK government signed declares that 'no one shall be denied the right to education'. Although the Convention is not legally binding in the UK, its effects have already been felt, for example, when Parliament banned corporal punishment from LEA schools in 1986.

'I CAN'T GET COMPLAINTS DEALT WITH'

Problem

Members of your school staff as well as parents frequently bring matters affecting the school to your attention. Over a time you realise that most of them – on the face of it – are to do with the way the head teacher is managing the school and its staff. When you bring them up at meetings the chair asks you to put everything in writing to the head teacher and not to hold up the meeting. This makes you pull your punches a little because the head is present.

When you finally get a reply, it asserts that the complaints are simply mistaken – and the chair agrees with the writer. Next time you write in confidence directly to your chair. You are astonished to receive a snooty reply from the head teacher telling you that the chair has passed your letter on, and that, again, there is no substance to the complaint.

Comment

Your chair was quite wrong to pass your confidential letter to the head teacher, but perhaps you didn't mark it 'confidential', you merely assumed such matters would be treated as such. The correct procedure would have been for the chair to make the necessary enquiries without mentioning your name and write back to you personally.

It sounds as if your governing body is suffering from a known complaint – a 'let's get it all sewn up between us' agreement by chair and head teacher. Such agreements are sometimes deodorised by using terms like 'smooth and efficient decision-making' or 'complete openness and trust between head teacher and governors'.

The symptoms of the problem are often that the chair and head teacher sit close to each other at meetings and that frequently one of them answers questions which governors have addressed to the other. They are also often personal friends and meet frequently socially. The chair will more frequently than is proper assert that such and such a matter 'is really the head teacher's business', implying that governors should not interfere.

If allowed to progress untreated, this problem causes governors to feel that going to meetings is a waste of time since all important matters are dealt with elsewhere. It can spread to other governors who are not really interested in the job and are actually glad that others are taking responsibility. If the governors live a long distance from the school they may be glad not to be too involved with the day to day running of the school. That is, until the heavenly duo make a bad mistake and the whole governing body is in trouble.

It is the governing body as a whole, not individual members of it, which makes decisions and must live with them. Behaviour of this sort must be remembered when the chair comes up for re-election. If complaints are received which might involve the head teacher, the chair should immediately inform the head teacher of them in a confidential manner, and then take steps to check independently of the head teacher.

The borderline between the legitimate business of the head teacher and that of the governors is a faint and delicate one. In an ideal world no one would talk defensively about demarcation. Some governors are guilty on occasion of too much wilful and unhelpful interference in the head teacher's work: others stand back too far from the school, fail to give proper support and take it out on the head teacher when things go wrong. Getting it right is not easy, and some governors are afraid to overstep the mark. There is a memorable phrase from Joan Sallis, however: 'I may not be a trained mechanic, but I know when my car is not running properly.'

A good idea is to hold an informal, unminuted meeting of governors to discuss the way meetings are run. For this meeting there is a discussion leader, not the chair or vice-chair. If members sit around a table or in a circle there is no 'top table' and all can say just what they think. Meetings like this are likely to be most successful after about the fourth formal meeting of a new governing body.

VANDALISM

Problem

Your school has been suffering from broken windows, particularly at the weekend, from graffiti and the theft of valuable equipment. At one time you could hope that the LEA might pick up the bills; nowadays it comes out of *your* budget. Insurance too is expensive: when you have been burgled more than once it becomes prohibitive.

Comment

Here are a few quick ideas.

- Ask members of staff if they would take valuable items of equipment home during holidays and at weekends. It is *vital*, however, that proper records are kept – in case the suspicion arises that members of staff have stolen them. Many teachers may understandably refuse, especially if it makes their house attractive to burglars. Check that your insurance policy covers possible loss when equipment is looked after by staff.
- Make sure that all equipment is security marked, with your postcode at the very least.
- Enlist the support of parents. Governors can be particularly helpful here. Vandalism is mostly caused by bored and idle children in the nearby community. Put vandalism prominently on the agenda for the annual meeting with parents.
- Would your parents be willing to exercise their dogs in the vicinity of the school? (Beware the penalties for fouling footpaths and playing fields!) The matter of local 'vigilantes' is a sensitive one, however, and such volunteers should *not* be encouraged to 'have a go'.
- Have a special 'graffiti wall' – give a small prize for the best and worst graffiti of the week or month? Risky, but at least it may concentrate efforts in one place.

- Neighbours and parents will sometimes be prepared to report vandals to teachers, but not to the police or caretakers. In small schools, particularly primary schools, parents and teachers often congregate at the school gates after school. Possibilities for intelligence work here.
- If parents supervise pupils on the school bus, they can often hear things of interest.

Care needs to be taken if vandals are reported to their school. If the school punishes them the punishment may be taken into consideration by the magistrates if the case later comes to court. There is a general principle that no one should be punished twice for the same offence. Indeed, if the school has dealt with the offence, the police may decide not to bring charges at all.

The position may be further complicated if the vandalism is to nearby property not belonging to the school. The magistrates can order the parents to compensate the victims; a school which, with the purest of intentions, threatens a pupil or a family with the police if compensation is not paid, may be doing something bordering on 'demanding money with menaces', itself a criminal offence.

BACK TO BASICS

Problem

Your school has been receiving complaints from parents and others that standards are slipping. Children are spending too much time 'messing about with unimportant things' and are not learning the basics. They are also less well behaved outside than they used to be. The head teacher argues that it is all a storm in a teacup and should be ignored.

Comment

It should definitely *not* be ignored. Rumours about schools rapidly get out of hand. Schools have learned from bitter experience that bad news for schools is good news for the media. Later retractions by the press are rarely if ever given the prominence of the original incorrect statements.

It would be useful to arrange a meeting for all parents with an inviting title such as 'How we try to educate your children at Ivyclad School', and allow plenty of time for questions. At the root of your difficulty is the fact that in recent years the school curriculum has changed so much and so rapidly that many parents, looking back to their own days at school, barely recognise it. This produces feelings of insecurity which schools should recognise and seek to calm. It sometimes helps at such meetings to invite a speaker of wide experience of schools and who clearly has no personal interest in your school.

Standards of behaviour are harder to deal with. Parents often talk of the stricter discipline of the teachers and schools of their youth and then, perhaps only minutes later, of the mayhem and disorder they created around them in youthful high spirits. That is by no means a new phenomenon.

It helps if parents and governors who are really concerned about so-called declining standards of behaviour try to describe just what they mean by 'good' and 'bad' behaviour. It will be seen immediately that only a very general agreement can be reached, because there will be so many dis-agreements. In seeking to accommodate one group of parents, your head teacher may have antagonised another. But if parents can give examples of the poor behaviour they have witnessed, at least that offers a start, though sometimes there may be more hearsay than evidence.

If governors remain concerned, then they can give their views on school discipline in writing formally to the head teacher, who should investigate them. If yours is an LEA school and your requirements cost money, the approval of the authority must be obtained.

FEELING OUT OF TOUCH

Problem

Some governors complain that they really know very little about their school. They meet only after school when there are no children around, and only occasionally see teachers and other staff apart from the cleaning and care-taking staff. The head teacher has invited them in but they are busy people at work all day and find it difficult to accept the invitations. They want to be more involved. They don't want to hold up meetings by asking for basic information about the school.

Comment

This is a long-standing problem. It may be fully resolved only when 'time off' to be a school governor is seen in the same light as time off to be a magistrate or to serve on a jury – as a vital public service. In the meanwhile the hours worked by devoted and unpaid men and women governors are indeed remarkable.

Some schools have a system of 'visiting governor(s)'. All governors take turns to be a general dogsbody for a shortish period, say a week, or a month. During that time the visiting governors deal with anything for which the school might need a governor. You might for example attend a staff meeting or two, attend all governors' sub-committee meetings, join in a school journey, sit in with the head teacher while parents are being interviewed (particularly prospective parents), chat with parents at the school gates or attend a meeting of the PTA. This is very effective on-the-job training, and a great morale booster for governors who are feeling rather out on a limb.

POLICE IN SCHOOL

Problem

A teacher has reported to the head that she has seen a 15-year-old pupil with some implements that she thinks may be used for drug-taking. The head agreed that this looks very suspicious. She first phoned the local police with whom the school has a good working relationship. She then immediately tried to phone the parents, but they seemed to be unavailable and the emergency contact number also did not reply. She phoned a neighbour and left a message asking the parents to contact the school. Within minutes the police arrived and interviewed the pupil in a quiet room nearby. After the police had left, the parents arrived and were angry that they had not been present during the interview.

Comment

This should not have happened. Your head was quite right to phone the police and the parents, but made the mistake of not holding up the pupil's interview with the police until the parents were present. A head teacher has authority to do so. If there were extreme circumstances, the head should have stood in for the parents during the interview.

All this is contained in police codes of conduct and LEA guidelines. By their action the police may have made it difficult for themselves to gain a conviction in court (if this is what they had in mind), because it is widely recognised that an interview conducted as this was, is unreliable and likely to put the pupil at a disadvantage.

THE STAFF WON'T CONDUCT THE NATIONAL TESTS

Problem

Teachers in your school are disgruntled, so they threaten to boycott the national tests or public examinations. The argument is partly about working conditions, since they feel that the tests are complicated and time-consuming. There is also a very strong undercurrent of disapproval of the tests themselves, and how much teaching time is taken from teaching to administer them. Some of your fellow governors are worried that, by not taking action, they could be seen to be condoning the teachers' 'strike'.

Comment

Many governors are concerned about this issue. It must be said at the outset that governors' *personal* views on the teachers' action and the tests are irrelevant here. The important facts to know are that:

- One of a teacher's tasks under the Baker contract mentioned elsewhere in this book is the 'assessing, recording and reporting on the development, progress and attainment of pupils'. Teachers, like any other employee, face disciplinary action if they fail to carry out their job fully. *In theory* teachers could have a deduction for 'partial fulfilment of contract' made from their salary; *in practice* it is hard to see how the deduction could be calculated.
- If governors take no action over disputes about National Curriculum tests, they will face real difficulty *if* the next professional 'target' turns out to be GCSE or A level.
- For serious breaches of contract, disciplinary action by employers under their school's disciplinary code is a distinct possibility. In grant maintained, independent, voluntary-aided schools and CTCs that means you as a governor. In LEA schools the responsibility may be divided between the governors and the LEA. Governors can't, however, sit back and pass the buck fully to their LEA.
- The head's contract requires him or her to see that the school runs properly. The head is also at risk if the school does not.
- If the Secretary of State receives a complaint from one of your parents about your failure to ensure that the tests run, he or she can come down heavily upon you as governors. Very nasty.

So much is clear. So, what happens if, despite all your efforts at negotiation, the staff remain adamant? Usually tests are *marked* externally, and in theory you could pay to *run* the tests with paid help from outside. You probably won't have budgeted for this, so you will have to weigh up whether the loss would be greater than the gain at any one time. It would certainly be a wise precaution to have a formally recorded discussion about this.

What you should not do *under any circumstances*, however your sympathies lie, is be seen to be supporting the teachers' action. To do so could bring real legal trouble, as it may start to look like 'conspiracy to break the law' or even 'secondary strike action'.

THE DIFFICULT TEACHER

Problem

A geography teacher at your school is very popular with both pupils and parents. His examination results are good and he gives unstintingly of his own time. His pupils have from time to time won national awards for their work in geography. As governors you have twice written to him commending him for his efforts on behalf of the pupils.

The problem is that he seems to regard himself as responsible only to his subject and his pupils. On several occasions he has failed to carry out scheduled supervision duties around your school: on one such occasion he was tracked down in his classroom introducing a fascinated group of younger pupils to fossils. He drives your school secretary mad by insisting that the photo-copying of material for his classes is done before anyone else's. Most recently he decided on impulse to take his sixth form pupils to visit a local waterfall, took the school's mini-bus and thereby almost ruined a theatre visit by another teacher and her group. He often does not turn up to staff meetings, and once departed for a national conference on geography two days before the end of term.

At one of your meetings the head tells you that he has had enough and has fired the teacher. Before doing so he consulted your chair and gained her approval. However the head also warns you that the teacher, supported by his union, is taking the matter to an industrial tribunal.

Comment

If we look back on our own schooldays we will probably recognise that we remember the *characters* who taught us rather than the *subjects* they taught. For all his infuriating behaviour this teacher may be one of *your* characters! Is there a chance of getting him to see the light, or have you reached the end of the road?

The teacher's behaviour is potentially dangerous. It is vitally important that school supervision duties are carried out efficiently. Pupils should never undertake school journeys without the prior approval of their parents or guardians. Failure in these respects can be a major problem if pupils are injured and there are actions for professional negligence, as we have noted elsewhere. If *any* employee disappears from his or her job without approval the employer is entitled to take disciplinary proceedings. Your head cannot manage the school without the co-operation of the staff. The teacher clearly has a problem in his attitude to all these critically important issues.

Except in the case of a few privately-owned and operated schools the head teacher is *not* the employer where dismissal is concerned: the governors are. Your head teacher almost certainly has no authority to issue dismissal notices, merely to suspend from school for good cause (on full salary) while the matter is referred to the governors for decision. Your head is not only wrong, but also unwise. If, for example (and we are all human), news had leaked out that he had dismissed wrongly and in a foul temper because he was at the end of his tether, the teacher for all his faults might have grounds for an action for defamation.

It looks as if your chair may have a lot to learn. She should have called an emergency meeting of your staffing sub-committee and put the matter to it. Assuming that the governors had formally delegated to that sub-committee the power to *start* dismissal proceedings, notice could then have been given to the teacher.

The teacher is entitled to an appeal to the governors against dismissal. As we noted earlier when discussing appeals by pupils against exclusion, the appeal must be heard by governors *who know nothing about what has happened already*. Members of the staffing sub-committee cannot therefore take part. The head and the teacher must present their cases.

In matters of dismissal the law insists that the correct procedures are carried out. Even if you have the strongest and most reasonable case for dismissing the teacher, the law will stop you if you follow the wrong procedures. The law cannot compel you to take the teacher back. If you refuse however he will be awarded compensation for 'unfair dismissal' as the law calls it. In a recent badly-handled case the compensation was around £20,000, which called into question the head's management skills, even though he was fundamentally in the right!

In cases like yours by far the better technique would have been to give the teacher, in writing, *a written warning* or a *final written warning*, spelling out what was required of him. If he re-offended – often the case with attitude problems – he could be dismissed on the spot and the governors would have been in the clear.

Not long ago a case came to light in an independent school where a teacher who had worked there for many years received a dismissal letter from the headmaster. The contract which the teacher had signed many years before contained the clause: 'The assistant teacher may be dismissed at the headmaster's pleasure.' The dismissal letter read: 'It gives me great pleasure to dismiss you.' Lawyers thrive on the back of such stupidity!!

BACK TO SCHOOL UNIFORM

Problem

The majority of governors of your school want to introduce school uniform. You have no strong views about this as a parent governor, but have the feeling that it would not be popular with other parents. You are worried that attempts to enforce the wearing of school uniform will create unnecessary strains between the school and parents.

Comment

Certainly it would not be a good idea to introduce school uniform without consulting parents. A letter inviting parents to a meeting about it before any decision is taken would be highly advisable. Many parents will be delighted at having uniforms. In fact, governors are not in general *obliged* to consult parents or staff before reaching their decisions, the argument being that those groups are in any case represented on the governing body. Opting out, of course, is an exception to this.

The worry about enforcement is well founded. As we noted before in connection with smoking, school rules are part of the law of the land. The question which all governors need to face therefore is: how far is your school prepared to go when Mrs Murgatroyd flatly refuses to send Sharon to school in uniform (that is, if she has any control anyway over anything Sharon does at 14)? The law is on governors' side – if it comes to the crunch, Sharon can be shown the door. But what governing body would rationally want to go so far?

The question of whether schools may take drastic action of this sort has been before the High Court in the 1950s and was decided in favour of schools. But if the matter came back to the courts in the 1990s we cannot be sure in the present climate that the court would take the same view over *uniform*. To make school uniform voluntary is probably the policy most likely to succeed.

'I THOUGHT THAT GOVERNORS' MEETINGS WERE SUPPOSED TO BE CONFIDENTIAL'

Problem

Our chair keeps bringing outsiders to meetings, in the interest of 'open government'. Usually they have very useful and helpful things to say, but I am worried that they may repeat things that they have heard, and that confidential matters will leak.

Comment

You are quite right. What is said at governors' meetings remains confidential. However, the minutes of meetings must be made available to parents at your school. The law on this point is sensible. No governor would feel able to speak freely if he or she knew that every comment would be repeated outside. And if a delicate personal problem affecting one of your families comes up for discussion, it would be most unfortunate and cruel if the subject were noised abroad. Some things which are said at meetings are incorrect, and other governors have to correct them. All governors are *representatives*, not *delegates*. A teacher governor, for example, is there to represent the interests of the teaching staff, not to carry back to the staff what has been said (except via the minutes).

The rules on confidentiality do not make it impossible for visitors to attend meetings. Visitors must however be invited *by the governing body as a whole*, and not by any governor acting on his or her own. The best procedure is to invite the visitor to attend only for the agenda item with which they are concerned and then to leave the meeting. As we mentioned in Chapter 2, if you want to hold some of your meetings in public, you will have to split your agenda into *unreserved* (public present) and *reserved* (public excluded) business, so as not to breach confidentiality.

BRINGING IN SOLICITORS

Problem

Our head teacher reported to us at the last meeting that she had temporarily excluded a girl for misbehaviour and had telephoned the parents to tell them what had happened. Within a couple of hours the father had appeared at the school with his solicitor who wanted to know what had happened and why. The head had not met this situation before, and, because the incident had taken place just before a governors' meeting, postponed the discussion with the parent and solicitor and asked your advice.

Comment

Heads and governors do not need to be over-concerned simply because solicitors come to school with parents. Parents sometimes need the support which legal help can offer, and there is no reason why schools should feel under threat if they do. The presence of a solicitor does not turn the meeting into a court of law with all the attendant complicated rules about evidence, hearsay and procedure. A head who knows what she is doing should behave to all intents and purposes exactly as if the solicitor were not there – in fact the legal adviser is really there to advise the parent, not run the meeting. It would be foolish of any school to jump to the conclusion that it had committed some error, simply because a solicitor was there: it is the lot of many a legal adviser to have to support *very* weak cases from time to time.

'TEACHER'S LOST MY TRANNY'

Problem

During a governors' meeting one of your colleagues brings up a delicate matter under 'Any other business'. She has received a complaint from Mr Jones that his son's transistor radio had been confiscated by a teacher after he was being a nuisance with it. When the boy went to collect it after school the teacher could not find it and said that it must have been stolen. Mr Jones had spoken to the head teacher about this: the head had said that the transistor had been a nuisance and that the teacher was right to confiscate it. The teacher was not responsible for its loss and compensation was out of the question.

Comment

Your colleague has not gone about this important matter in the right way. She is certainly entitled to bring up anything she likes under 'Any other business', but she has tried in effect to turn a governors' meeting into a trial of the head teacher's behaviour, which is not likely to go down well. The better way to do it would have been to take the matter first to the chair (or referred Mr Jones directly to the chair) and let the chair decide whether to put the matter on the agenda. If an issue goes on the agenda it is of course minuted – even if the whole thing turns out to be rubbish.

Nevertheless the head teacher seems to have misunderstood the legal position. The teacher is certainly not responsible for everything a pupil takes to school: he might not even be aware that Mary's pen is solid gold and came from Harrods, nor can he be expected to know. But this teacher did what any parent would have done by confiscating the nuisance. In this case the law says that the teacher must take as much care with it as he would with his own property. The law does not say that he must make good the loss: the parents must prove that the teacher was careless with it. This is likely to be difficult.

As governors it is open to you to consider a payment without admitting any responsibility. We would advise, though, that it would be undesirable. If the child had lost PE kit or a coat from the cloakroom we would have been more sympathetic. A transistor radio is not needed at school. Indeed, the cause of the trouble in the first place was that it was intentionally disruptive.

Chapter 8

Now that you're a good school governor

There is more to being a good school governor than reading a book about it. The quiz below is lighthearted, but also slightly serious. It is certainly not a properly validated test, merely a set of questions about being a governor. Score one point each time you answer (hand on heart!) 'yes', or give a correct answer which can be verified from local knowledge or reference to this book.

If you score 0 or 1 on any section you may need to take positive steps to improve in this area. If you score 4 or 5 you are possibly very good in that area, a dab hand at magazine quizzes, lucky, or a bit of a fibber.

A CURRICULUM

1 Have you read any curriculum statement prepared by the school in recent times?
2 Do you know if the school operates through separate subjects, or on blocks of time for integrated project and topic work, or both?
3 Have you looked at any textbooks in use in the school?
4 Do you know what the school does for the very able and for slow learners?
5 Can you say what the school is doing about new technology, like microcomputers etc.?

B TEACHERS AND TEACHING

1 Have you talked to any teachers in the school about their views on current issues in education?
2 Do you know what sort of in-service courses teachers in the school have been attending?
3 Have you talked informally to the head about teaching in the school and such matters as teacher appraisal?
4 Do you know how teachers monitor and assess pupils' progress?
5 Have you asked teachers what difficulties they may be facing, or what they may need to do their job more effectively?

C PARENTS AND COMMUNITY

1 Have you ever asked parents what they like and dislike about the school?
2 Have you ever attended a parents' meeting?
3 Have you visited different parts of the school's catchment area?
4 Do you know what jobs parents in the area do, or what level of unemployment there is?
5 Are you aware of the use made of the school's premises outside normal hours by members of the community?

D CHILDREN

1 Have you talked to any children in the school (other than your own if you're a parent governor)?
2 Have you been to watch any of the children's plays, concerts or sports?
3 Have you looked at any of the children's work, on display or anywhere else?
4 Do you know how the school handles children with learning or behaviour problems?
5 Do you know what leisure interests children in the school enjoy?

E ORGANISATION

1 Do you know how decisions are made in the school about policy and curriculum?
2 Do you know the names of your fellow governors?
3 Have you ever attended a meeting of your local education committee?
4 Could you understand a simple financial statement about your school's budget?
5 Would you know how to get an item put on the agenda of your governors' meeting?

F ACTION

1 If an urgently needed building project were continually deferred, would you know what action to take?
2 Are you willing to 'get things moving' if governors' meetings become tedious or pointless?
3 If your school were threatened with closure, would you know what to do?
4 Have you ever volunteered to do something at a governors' meeting?
5 Do you tend to participate in most governors' meetings and not continually defer to the chair or head?

Scores (out of 5)   *Points*
A Curriculum   ....
B Teachers and teaching   ....
C Parents and community   ....
D Children   ....
E Organisation   ....
F Action   ....

                                         Total   ————

TOTAL SCORE

25–30 You must frighten the life out of your fellow governors, the head and staff. Do you ever pause for breath, say hello to the budgie or your family, or for that matter tell the truth in magazine quizzes?

18–24 Congratulations, you are a black belt governor. Two or three like you and your school will get all the resources going.

7–17 You are probably strong in some areas and weaker in others. See if you need to work at aspects where you obtained a low score.

1–6 If you are a new governor you have probably not yet had time to learn about the school, but if you have been a governor for several years, ask yourself how you can be more effective.

0 Resign, but only after checking your pulse. You may have passed away at a boring governors' meeting and been allowed to stay on posthumously.

Teachers' Pay and Conditions Document:

Conditions of Employment of School Teachers

PART XI – CONDITIONS OF EMPLOYMENT OF TEACHERS OTHER THAN HEAD TEACHERS

Exercise of general professional duties

35. A teacher who is not a head teacher shall carry out the professional duties of a teacher as circumstances may require:

35.1 if he is employed as a teacher in a school, under the reasonable direction of the head teacher of that school;

35.2 if he is employed by an authority on terms under which he is not assigned to any one school, under the reasonable direction of that authority and of the head teacher of any school in which he may for the time being be required to work as a teacher.

Exercise of particular duties

36.1 A teacher employed as a teacher (other than a head teacher) in a school shall perform, in accordance with any directions which may reasonably be given to him by the head teacher from time to time, such particular duties as may reasonably be assigned to him.

36.2 A teacher employed by an authority on terms such as those described in paragraph 35.2 shall perform, in accordance with any direction which may reasonably be given to him from time to time by the authority or by the head teacher of any school in which he may for the time being be required to work as a teacher, such particular duties as may reasonably be assigned to him.

Professional duties

37. The following duties shall be deemed to be included in the professional duties which a teacher (other than a head teacher) may be required to perform:

37.1 Teaching:

In each case having regard to the curriculum for the school:

37.1.1 planning and preparing courses and lessons;

37.1.2 teaching, according to their educational needs, the pupils assigned to him, including the setting and marking of work to be carried out by the pupil in school and elsewhere;

37.1.3 assessing, recording and reporting on the development, progress and attainment of pupils;

37.2 Other activities:

37.2.1 promoting the general progress and well-being of individual pupils and of any class or group of pupils assigned to him;

37.2.2 providing guidance and advice to pupils on educational and social matters and on their further education and future careers, including information about sources of more expert advice on specific questions; making relevant records and reports;

37.2.3 making records of and reports on the personal and social needs of pupils;

37.2.4 communicating and consulting with the parents of pupils;

37.2.5 communicating and co-operating with persons or bodies outside the school; and

37.2.6 participating in meetings arranged for any of the purposes described above;

37.3 Assessments and reports:

providing or contributing to oral and written assessments, reports and references relating to individual pupils and groups of pupils;

37.4 Appraisal:

participating in arrangements made in accordance with The Education (School Teacher Appraisal) Regulations 1991 (SI 1991/1511) for the appraisal of his performance and that of other teachers;

37.5 Review: further training and development:

37.5.1 reviewing from time to time his methods of teaching and programmes of work; and

37.5.2 participating in arrangements for his further training and professional development as a teacher;

37.6 Educational methods:

advising and co-operating with the head teacher and other teachers (or any one or more of them) on the preparation and development of courses of study, teaching materials, teaching programmes, methods of teaching and assessment and pastoral arrangements;

37.7 Discipline, health and safety:

maintaining good order and discipline among the pupils and safeguarding their health and safety both when they are authorised to be on the school premises and when they are engaged in authorised school activities elsewhere;

37.8 Staff meetings:

participating in meetings at the school which relate to the curriculum for the school or the administration or organisation of the school, including pastoral arrangements;

37.9 Cover

37.9.1 Subject to paragraph 37.9.2, supervising and so far as practicable teaching any pupils whose teacher is not available to teach them:

37.9.2 Subject to the exceptions in paragraph 37.9.3, no teacher shall be required to provide such cover:

(a) after the teacher who is absent or otherwise not available has been so for three or more consecutive working days; or
(b) where the fact that the teacher would be absent or otherwise not available for a period exceeding three consecutive working days was known to the maintaining authority or, in the case of a grant-maintained or grant-maintained special school or a school which has a delegated budget and whose local management scheme delegates to the governing body the relevant responsibility for the provision of supply teachers, to the governing body for two or more working days before the absence commenced;

37.9.3 The exceptions are:

(a) he is a teacher employed wholly or mainly for the purpose of providing such cover ('a supply teacher'); or
(b) the authority or the governing body (as the case may be) have exhausted

all reasonable means of providing a supply teacher to provide cover without success; or

(c) he is a full-time teacher at the school but has been assigned by the head teacher in the time-table to teach or carry out other specified duties (except cover) for less than 75 per cent of these hours in the week during which pupils are taught at the school;

37.10 Public examinations:

participating in arrangements for preparing pupils for public examinations and in assessing pupils for the purposes of such examinations; recording and reporting such assessments; and participating in arrangements for pupils' presentation for and supervision during such examinations;

37.11 Management:

37.11.1 contributing to the selection for appointment and professional development of other teachers and non-teaching staff, including the induction and assessment of new and probationary teachers;

37.11.2 co-ordinating or managing the work of other teachers; and

37.11.3 taking such part as may be required of him in the review, development and management of activities relating to the curriculum, organisation and pastoral functions of the school;

37.12 Administration

37.12.1 participating in administrative and organisational tasks related to such duties as are described above, including the management or supervision of persons providing support for the teachers in the school and the ordering and allocation of equipment and materials; and

37.12.2 attending assemblies, registering the attendance of pupils and supervising pupils, whether these duties are to be performed before, during or after school sessions.

Working time

38.1 A teacher employed full-time, other then in the circumstances described in paragraph 38.3, shall be available for work for 195 days in any school year, of which 190 days shall be days on which he may be required to teach pupils in addition to carrying out other duties; and those 195 days shall be specified by his employer or, if the employer so directs, by the head teacher.

38.2 Such a teacher shall be available to perform such duties at such times and such places as may be specified by the head teacher (or, where the teacher is not assigned to any one school, by his employer or the head teacher of any school in which he may for the time being be required to work as a teacher) for 1265 hours in any school year, those hours to be allocated reasonably throughout those days in the school year on which he is required to be available for work.

38.3 Paragraphs 38.1 and 38.2 do not apply to such a teacher employed wholly or mainly to teach or perform other duties in relation to pupils in a residential establishment.

38.4 Time spent in travelling to or from the place of work shall not count against the 1265 hours referred to in paragraph 38.2.

38.5 Such a teacher shall not be required under his contract as a teacher to undertake midday supervision, and shall be allowed a break of reasonable length either between school sessions or between the hours of 12 noon and 2.00pm.

38.6 Such a teacher shall, in addition to the requirements set out in paragraphs 38.1 and 38.2, work such additional hours as may be needed to enable him to discharge effectively his professional duties, including, in particular, the marking of pupils' work, the writing of reports on pupils and the preparation of lessons, teaching material and teaching programmes. The amount of time required for this purpose beyond the 1265 hours referred to paragraph 38.2 and the times outside the 1265 specified hours at which duties shall be performed shall not be defined by the employer but shall depend upon the work needed to discharge the teacher's duties.

Select bibliography

BOOKS

Bush, T., Coleman, C. and Glover, M. *Managing Autonomous Schools*, Paul Chapman Publishing, June 1993. A research survey of the early days of 100 grant-maintained schools.

Dodds, N. and King, G., *Developing Effective Policies*, Governor Teacher Presentations, King's House, St John's Square, Wolverhampton WV2 4DT. A series of seven mini-guides on preparing the documentation which all schools today must have. Topics include the annual report to parents and the school prospectus.

Griffiths, A. and Hamilton, D., *Parent, Teacher, Child*, Methuen, 1984.

Lowe, C. J., *The School Governor's Legal Guide*, Croner Publications, 1988. A handy and compact guide to intricacies.

Lowe, C. J., *Hobson's School Travel Organiser's UK Handbook*, Hobson's Publishing, 1989. Useful for advice on the increasingly tricky area of running school journeys.

Mahoney, T., *Governing Schools: Powers, Issues and Practice*, Macmillan Education, 1988. A well-written and lively book, good on specific issues such as sexism.

Partington, J. A. and Wragg, E. C., *Schools and Parents*, Cassell, 1989. An easy-to-read guide for parents. Knowing how parents see schools is vital for school governors.

School Governor's Manual, Croner Publications, 1989. The full legal background to being a governor. Published in loose-leaf format with a regular updating service. Every governing body should keep one handy. Has a very useful monthly magazine also (see below).

Sallis, J., *School Governors – A Question and Answer Guide Answered*, Butterworth Heinemann, 1995. Very readable answers to a large number of questions sent in by school governors to the *Times Educational Supplement*.

Sallis, J., *The Effective School Governor*, Advisory Centre for Education, 1993.

Sallis, J., *Schools, Parents and Governors*, Routledge, 1990.

MAGAZINES

Managing Schools Today, Questions Publishing Company, 27 Frederick Street, Hockley, Birmingham B1 3HH. A leading regular magazine useful for governors and all staff in management of schools. Highly recommended.

Governors' Action, Action for Governors' Information and Training (see below).

School Governor's Briefing, Croner Publications, Kingston on Thames. A very useful monthly newsletter to subscribers to Croner's loose-leaf *School Governor's Manual*.

USEFUL ORGANISATIONS

Advisory Centre for Education, 18 Victoria Park Square, London E2 9PB: *A Governor's Handbook*. Straightforward to read and inexpensive.

Department for Education: *Governors' Guide to the Law*. Comes free of charge, loose-leaf, with a regular up-dating service. *Education (School Governing Bodies) Regulations 1989*. Reports on inspections of schools (HMI and OFSTED).

Action for Governors' Information and Training, Lyng Hall, Blackberry Lane, Coventry CV2 3JS.

National Association of Governors and Managers, Christopher Hatton Centre, 26 Laystall Street, London EC1R 4PQ.

National Governors' Council, Glebe House, Church Street, Crediton, Devon EX17 2AF.

Index